Peaceful-Golf

A Journey Into The Unknown

by

Noah Pilipski

Editors: Jennifer Obolewicz and Kim Kleinle
Designed by Christopher Derrick exclusively for Unauthrized Media

ISBN-10: 1633188523
ISBN-13: 9781633188525

AUTHOR'S NOTE

Certain names and dates have been changed to protect people's privacy

CHAPTER 1

In the middle of difficulty lies opportunity
– Albert Einstein

My first memories of golf begin with my father. He was a foreman at a scene shop in Newburg, New York, that made sets for Broadway shows. He spent most of his time working, so the little free time he had was spent with family or golfing. I was around four years-old when he decided it was time for me to learn the game. He cut down the shafts of an old set of ladies clubs that he bought at the flea market. He then wrapped duct tape around the shafts to make the grips. I thought this was really cool—not so much the clubs but the fact that I could now spend time with the man I loved the most, my dad.

Dad thought he would show me the "basics" of the swing and let me have at it. The only problem was that the basics I learned were the same bad habits he had taught himself. Right away I developed a terrible slice, which stuck with me until the age of twenty-three. I came to fear the slice, and thus my swing became more and more tense. Not something you ever want in your golf swing.

Some of the best memories are from my time playing golf with my father. We would have some epic matches that usu-

ally ended with me in tears. I wanted to impress my father, so I always tried as hard as I could. As you will learn, golf—or anything really—doesn't work too well when you use excess force. As a young strong boy, easing up wasn't even an option. Fortunately, I picked up the game pretty quickly and was shooting around 110 by the time I was eight or nine years-old, even with my slice. By the time I was eleven, I wanted to try some tournament golf. I remember asking my friend Adam to caddie for me, and he agreed eagerly. I was the only guy in the tournament with a caddie. I got the caddie idea from my father, who as a young man was a caddie and a groundskeeper at the famed Concord Monster Golf Course in Kiamesha Lake, New York. My dad used to tell me great stories about the course and his work on it. For some reason, I just loved hearing them.

So there I was, eleven years old, playing in my first tourney ever, caddie in tow and a smile from ear to ear. I was playing in Port Jervis, New York, at a private club built by the famed architect A.W. Tillinghast. This was indeed a rare treat for me. We usually played on municipal tracks. My family was not poor but pretty damn close. My father came from nothing and was determined to work his way out of poverty. To his credit, he pulled us out of poverty and in the process, set a great example for me. From the time when I was very young, my father and mother instilled in me a sense of my own value— that I could truly be whatever I wanted. Settling was not an option.

On the first tee of the tournament, I met my playing partners: an eighth-grader named John, who was nearly twice my size, and a little fellow named Eugene. Off we went down the first hole, and I was doing great. We all stayed even par until the fifth hole, when John started hitting into all kinds of trouble. The kid must have taken twelve strokes on this one hole alone. It's common practice in tournament golf to keep the score of your opponent and vice versa, making cheating on the score nearly impossible, or so I thought. At the end of the fifth hole, John said to Eugene, who was keeping his score, "I got a 7." Eugene, without flinching, said "OK!" Being super competitive, I was not having it. I said, "7? More like a 12."

John looked at me with the most intimidating stare and said very firmly, "I said 7." Yes, I was competitive, but I was also painfully aware that John was six feet-tall and weighed more than Adam and I combined. I was no dummy. The conversation was over. I was steaming over the incident, and to make matters worse, John did it four more times during the round. He was outright cheating. Adam was just as distraught as I was. "Why is he doing this?" asked Adam. I had no answer.

After the round was over I saw why. John was the winner and two-time champion. He received a huge trophy and everyone smiled and talked to him. I was devastated. I knew I had beaten John, but unfortunately only Adam and Eugene knew the truth. I lost all interest in playing tournament golf. That one experience had a long and lasting effect on me. If competition made people behave in this way; was competition something I really wanted to be a part of?

As the years went by, I found other things in life that took me away from golf, but I still enjoyed hitting the links with my father from time to time. Dad was always telling me I should work harder on my golf game because it might open doors to other opportunities. Being a typical teenager, I didn't want any advice from my parents about what I should or should not do with my life. I was cocky and thought I had all the answers. Golf wasn't cool. At least not in my eyes. What I wanted was to be a football player. The only problem with that was my parents wouldn't let me play. I am sure you can image the conflict this created. It was as if my parents somehow knew what was best for me! Ah, the nerve of them! As a curious and eager thirteen-year-old, I wanted what I wanted and was focused on my own self interests. I was also oblivious

to the fact that my mother and father had begun experiencing some tough times in their relationship. My father had quit his job as the shop foreman and decided to travel the country for a year with the Broadway show "Sweet Charity" as the assistant carpenter. He would be on the road for about six months to get the show going and then my mom, my sister, and I would join him in San Fransisco, where we would live and go to school for six months. I thought this was really cool, and I was excited about the new adventure. The three of us started driving across country to a city I had never seen. The longest trip I had ever taken before was to Washington, D.C., so this journey was a big deal.

After a two-week road trip, we finally arrived in San Francisco at our new home, a decent-sized apartment in a complex located on Lake Merced. The area is the home of two really amazing golf courses: TPC Harding Park and the famed Olympic Club, which was right behind my new apartment building. The Olympic Club is a private club that has hosted the U.S. Open three times, the most memorable in 1955 when Jack Fleck beat Ben Hogan in an 18-hole playoff.

My first few weeks in this big new city took a little getting used to. I was now attending one of the larger public schools in San Fransisco. My hometown school in Port Jervis had only 300 students in the entire school. So this would be a totally different experience for me. I managed to adapt well and within no time I was making friends and having a great time. By chance, one day I was on the playground enjoying a game of handball when a boy I had just met, Louis, started telling me how he worked right near my house. He was a caddie at the Olympic Club and said if I wanted he could probably get me a job there, too. Oh wow—this sounded so cool! Now I could be a caddie just like my dad. I really wanted to do this, and the best part was the course was a stone's throw from my home.

That day I ran home to ask my mom if I could go to the

club and see about a job. Surprisingly, she said yes! Louis had told me of a secret trail right behind my house, so I wouldn't even need a ride to the course—I could just walk there. When I finally got to the caddie shack, Louis was waiting outside. He took me straight in and introduced me to the caddie master, who looked me over and said, "Can you carry two bags for 18 holes?"

My response was a quick, "Yes, sir, no problem." Of course, I had never carried any full-size bag for 18 holes, let alone two. But that minor detail wasn't going to stop me from getting the job.

At home, I kept my set of six clubs in a super light canvas bag—nothing like the huge, heavy staff bags at Olympic Club. The caddie master agreed to let me work as long as I stayed out of the way and paid attention. For the next two weeks, I went every day and sat on the caddie bench waiting in anticipation for my first loop. The caddie master had me do mundane tasks like cleaning clubs, polishing shoes, sweeping the shop and basically everything except carrying a bag. After the third week, it became obvious I was never going to get out, at least not in the foreseeable future. What a disappointment. I felt really let down. All the action was on the course—why wasn't I allowed to be a part of it?

After our six months in San Francisco was up, my family returned home to Westbrookville, New York. Never getting a loop was constantly on my mind, but that was the least of my problems. My parents were having some real issues with their marriage and decided to get a divorce. I was asked who I wanted to live with—a choice no child wants to make, but one that I was forced to make nonetheless. Being really close to my mother and having not seen my dad much growing up, I chose to go with my mother. We moved to a little town called Monticello, about thirty miles from Westbrookville. The heyday of Monticello (from "Dirty Dancing" fame) was the 1950s, when it was a bustling little town with quaint shops

and summer hotels that attracted people seeking to escape the noisy, busy city life of Manhattan. By the time we moved there, it was just a bunch of rundown hotels with almost no business. In all honesty, it was a bit depressing. A couple of factors contributed to the decline of this area. Gambling was set to be legalized in the area, but when Atlantic City casinos opened their doors and the state of New York said no to gambling, any hope for new construction and updates in Monticello were gone. This was also about the time air travel started becoming affordable for most Americans, which meant instead of heading to the Catskills, people could explore the world. These factors, among others, led to the whole area becoming one of the poorest regions in all of New York state.

The one attraction the area did have because of the giant resort hotels was incredible world-class championship golf. These courses were so good that the PGA Tour, in its early years, included tour stops there. Players like Sam Snead, Ben Hogan, and Arnold Palmer, just to name a few, all cashed checks there. The tracks were generally mountain courses with incredible views and scenery: Grossingers Country Club, Kutcher's, the Nevele, and of course the Concord, with its two courses, the International and the world-famous Monster. My high school was only three miles from the Concord Resort. This really didn't mean much to me at the time, though. I was more interested in playing football, remember? The only problem, besides the fact that neither my mother nor father would sign the permission slip, was the lack of a football team at Monticello High School. About ten years earlier, a young boy was killed while playing football, so the school could no longer afford the insurance to have a team.

With no chance to play football, I was forced to look elsewhere for my sports fix. Recently divorced and a single parent, my mother was trying to get her footing on her own. She decided to take a job tending bar at one of the local muni golf courses called Wooded Glenn Golf Club. We didn't have much money, so my after-school program was to go out on the golf course and play until dark. I really enjoyed golf during this period of my life. My swing was a free action, void of any real instruction. I had no idea what a swing plane was or whether I was coming from the inside or not. All I knew was golf seemed like something I was getting better at. After getting my score down to around 95, I decided to join the golf team. I'm not totally sure why I joined other than I wanted to play some free golf and see what competitive golf had to offer me this time around.

Gary Woodmaker, the head pro where my mom worked, took a liking to me and lent me a set of clubs to use while I was on the team. These were the sweetest clubs I had ever seen—Ram forged irons! Needless to say, forged irons are probably not the best clubs for a fifteen-year-old, but they will teach you about hitting the sweet spot. You see, a golf club has a very small area that will actually produce consistent golf shots. The size of this sweet spot is about the size of a penny, directly in the center of the club's face. The part of the golf ball that compresses when hit is also the size of a penny. So what this really means is: You are trying to match two pennies perfectly together at over 100 mph. Hopefully, this gives you an idea how hard this game really is. Trying to use eye-hand coordination to strike at the ball is very difficult—so difficult, in fact, that many great athletes with superior eye-hand coordination never learn to play golf at a high level. This was my problem. I kept trying to match the pennies or hit the ball with my hands and arms, what I would call steering the clubhead consciously.

So with clubs in hand and being the newcomer on the golf team, I headed to my first practice, which was really just us playing nine holes of golf on the International course at the Concord. After my first practice round, I felt pretty good. I made a few good shots and even started becoming comfortable with the forged irons. Then day two of practice began. I

got to the approach shot on the first hole and realized I had lost my 8 iron. This was a big deal. My mom's boss lent me those clubs. They were his personal sticks, not some flea market set. This guy was a pro, not some hack! As you can imagine, the missing 8 iron stressed me out tremendously. My mind and body were in a complete state of nervousness, and I could not stop thinking about the fact that I lost Gary's club. That round ended horribly and so did the rest of the six matches I had that season. All I could think about was losing that 8 iron. Would my mom get fired? Would I be looked upon as untrustworthy? What did all this worry get me? Nothing. Gary never asked me for the set of clubs back. In fact, after the season was over, he told me to keep them and enjoy the game for the rest of my life. My experience with those clubs from Gary taught me a valuable lesson about caring for other people's things and how thought could ruin your game.

That was my last season of high school golf. I had gotten a car and a girlfriend, which meant golf was taking a back seat. That's not to say I never played. My father and I would get out a handful of times a year and a few buddies would call me to join them occasionally to play, but all in all, golf was nearly the last thing on my mind.

CHAPTER 2

Knowing yourself is the beginning of wisdom
– Aristotle

I SUPPOSE IT was about two years after high school that golf found its way back into my life. I had finished high school and was expected to go to college. And that's exactly what I did. After my first semester at college, I decided it was not the path for me and asked my father to help me get a job interview for a position building Broadway scenery. My father got me the interview and I got the job. Nepotism at its finest. A few weeks went by and my father asked me to come play golf with him. I said sure why not, even though it had been at least six months since I picked up a club. We went to the Fallsview resort in Ellenville, New York. This course was built by Robert Trent Jones Sr. and was a stern test of golf even though it was only nine holes. On the very first hole in the middle of the fairway, my father asked me, "What are you going to do with your life?"

At that instant, as if a thunderbolt hit me from above, I looked at him point blank and said, "I'm going to be a professional golfer." I don't know why I said it. I wasn't any good, I hadn't played in years, and I never showed any real interest in golf. So this statement caught both my father and me a bit off guard. My father laughed a little and brushed it off. But I

was serious and I didn't know why. All I knew was it sure felt right. I was nineteen years old, and for once in my life I felt like I had a direction.

As exciting and enlightening as this realization was, I didn't have any idea how to start the process, so I figured let's play golf! A lot of golf. This was my approach. I befriended a decent golfer named Tom Stellar. Tom was my age and was about my level in skill. We started playing every chance we could. Tom and I played at least three days a week, and within only a few months, I was consistently in the low 90s, which in my eyes was great, especially since I never really practiced until now. Only twenty or thirty shots to shave off. Easy task. Or so I thought. How hard could this be? Little did I know what golf had in store for me.

About four years later, the time came in my professional theater career when I was offered a job traveling the country with the Broadway show "How To Succeed In Business Without Really Trying," starring Ralph Macchio, the Karate Kid himself. I took the job without hesitation, with the intention of practicing my game more during the off time. Broadway shows are at night, so I would be free during the day to play as much golf as I wanted. Another great aspect of touring was that I would be moving to a new city every two weeks. Every city was a whole new set of golf courses to play and learn from. Life was amazing. I was twenty-three years old, had a great job and was free to work on my golf game.

There was only one problem: My golf game wasn't progressing as I had hoped. I still stunk at this game. A score of 95 was common and 90 was a miracle. Hoping to improve, I played golf all the time and would go to resorts on my days off, playing courses like Pebble Beach, Black Wolf Run and many others. Once I even stayed overnight in the clubhouse at Pebble Beach, just to make sure I was first off the next day. The more I played, the more I started looking for different swing techniques in the hopes of getting better. In Dallas,

I took a lesson at the Hank Haney Golf Ranch, and in San Francisco, I took lessons from Justin Leonard's swing coach. I went to so many driving range pros, I lost count. Each one of them seemed to have a different idea about how to swing the club. I became more and more disillusioned with the golf swing. It seemed the more I practiced, the worse I became.

Most of the time, I chose the courses I played by using the Golf Digest "Places To Play" book. The book rated golf courses from 0 to 5 stars and included comments and stats about each course. I tried to play all the 4 and 5-star courses I could. One day in Tampa Bay, Florida, while flipping through the Golf Digest book, I found a new golf facility called World Woods, about 70 miles north of Tampa and designed by Tom Fazio, a golf architect I had yet to hear of. The facility had two courses, both completely different from each other. Rolling Oaks is a beautiful parkland style course winding through the woods with some great rolling terrain. In contrast, Pine Barrens is target golf at its best. Sand is everywhere, and it's not considered a hazard, so you can ground your club anywhere. When I played these courses in the late 1990s, both were ranked on the Golf Digest top 100 list and still are today. For all the accolades the courses received, I struggled more than usual. I shot a 96 on Rolling Oaks and was about to finish worse on Pine Barrens. Finishing up the last hole of the day, I remember saying to myself, "I'm done! My game is terrible and the more I practice the worse I get." Maybe the feeling I had that day with my dad years ago was wrong. Maybe this was all just a young man grasping at straws. All I knew was something had to change or I wasn't going to be playing golf anymore.

As I finished the round, I decided to head to the pro shop and buy a hat and shirt with the course logo. The pro shop was small and understated, reminding me of the one at Spyglass Hill in Monterey. As I began to look around the shop, I spotted a small hardcover yellow book on one of the shelves.

The title was "Gravity Golf—The Evolution and Revolution of Golf Instruction." I had never seen this book before even though I had researched and studied golf for quite some time. I asked the gentleman behind the counter if he knew anything about the book. He replied that he knew all about it because the author, David Lee, gave instruction at the course. David taught a very unique and different approach to the game. The gentleman told me that David taught people to hop around on one foot as a way to learn to hit the golf ball, as well as some other strange drills. I asked the gentleman if the technique worked. He responded with a sarcastic, "You tell me. They are hopping around on one foot." Even though this technique did sound a little strange, I was intrigued. As I was thumbing through the first few pages, I came across a quote that caught my eye:

"The GRAVITY teaching system can take a player from a complete beginner to a competitive level professional in a period as short as twelve to eighteen months."

I decided to buy the book because no one else had promised results like those in such a short time. That night I read the book cover to cover, and when I finished, I couldn't wait to get to the range.

First thing the next morning I was at the range raring to go. I started with the infamous one-footed drill with a 6 iron. I took my stance, balanced on my front leg, and took a rip. On the downswing, I still felt like this new swing might work … right up until the point when I missed the ball completely. It was shortly after that when I felt myself losing balance and the hard sensation of my butt hitting the ground. I had just ripped myself off the ground and fell right back to it. This was going to be way harder than it looked in the pictures.

After about a half-hour and no success, I decided to try a new drill, one of the first drills David ever discovered—the "transfer drill" or "baseball drill." When I tried this drill for the first time, I crushed it! I hit my first ball over the driving range fence, which was only about 250 yards, but it was still farther than I had been hitting it. I was ecstatic. I needed to see this in action, so I grabbed my clubs and headed to the course. Once I got there, my super long drives were nowhere to be found. Instead, I found intense tension in my swing. It seemed that the golf course brought out tension that the driving range did not. It wasn't until the third hole that I finally got a hold of one. I hit the ball with my feet moving like a baseball pitcher throwing from the mound. I hit this ball so hard and so straight it sounded like a bullet coming out of a gun. I drove straight down the fairway looking for the ball. Unfortunately, I couldn't find it anywhere. Considering that the hole wasn't very long—maybe only 285 yards with no trouble anywhere—I thought it would be easy to find. Five minutes later, there was still no ball in sight. This was getting ridiculous. "I finally hit a good shot and I can't even find it!" I said aloud to myself. I took a penalty, dropped a ball and played the hole out. I was a beaten man. This game had caused me enough pain. I was ready to give up. As I pulled to the next tee, there was my ball—my tee shot from the previous hole—sitting right in the middle of the box. I had hit the ball almost three hundred yards! I was sold. My swing now had some power, and it felt amazing. Let's do more of this Gravity Golf!

CHAPTER
3

I will prepare and someday my chance will come
– Abraham Lincoln

FOR THE NEXT year, I immersed myself in Gravity Golf and continuously practiced all the drills. I wasn't the best by any means, but I wasn't afraid to try. Everything David Lee spoke about seemed to ring true. I continued practicing the Gravity Golf method and began making some real progress. This was not to say everything was peaches and cream. The golf swing is a living, breathing thing and words are a poor description for what is really going on. David described things that were open for interpretation, things like relaxed arms and tension. How relaxed is relaxed and should I be limp like a noodle? Questions like this often got me very confused. I realized that the only person who could answer these questions for me was David Lee himself. Since the first time I read David's book, I knew one day I would need to go and meet this man and ask him to train me. He was a very well-known teacher among tour pros and had a reputation for being a bit eccentric in his approach to the game, but he did have some real success. Chi Chi Rodriguez believed so much in David's method that he sent his own nephew to train with him. Lee Trevino, well known for saying he "would never take a lesson from a pro who couldn't beat him," ended up giving David a check for a golf lesson, saying David Lee was the only man alive who knew his swing and how it worked as well as Trevino himself did. Rocky Thompson, another distinguished student of David's, shot a 61 in the final round of the Tampa Open, which at that time was the lowest final round in senior tour history. After winning the event, Rocky said he owed the round to David Lee, who gave him a lesson on the range just before he teed off. Another great who had taken lessons from David Lee was none other than Mr. Jack Nicklaus himself. You could see why I felt David Lee was the guy for me. I mean, if he was good enough for Jack Nicklaus, then he was probably good enough for me!

During that whole year of training, I kept telling my family that once I had become truly proficient at these drills I was going to see David Lee and ask him to train me full time. I had saved some money and was ready to take the next step in my golf career. I finally felt I was as far as I could take myself by just using his book. I decided to take a week's vacation from work and call David Lee about booking a three-day golf school. Unfortunately, when I called, his secretary, who I later learned was his wife Cricket, informed me that David would not be teaching anymore this year, but I could go to one of his other very qualified instructors. I thanked her but told her it was only David Lee I was interested in seeing. She said if anything opened up she would call me and let me know. This was, to say the least, a bit frustrating. But then, out of nowhere, two weeks later I got a call from Cricket saying that David had to give a golf school to someone who won a contest. If I wanted, I could join that school. I instantly said, "I'll be there!" and booked my ticket for Hot Springs, Arkansas.

David Lee grew up in Hot Springs and was the captain of the golf team at the University of Arkansas. He played on the PGA Tour in the 1970s and now had golf schools in Florida, California and Hot Springs, Arkansas. The town is the site of a national park, and tourism is a huge part of its economy. It

reminded me of the Lake George region in upstate New York. There was a huge man-made lake called Lake Hamilton, and bridges seemed to be everywhere. I arrived late in the evening, so I wasn't able to drive over to see David's facility until the next morning. I found a small local motel that night, right on the lake, and had a good night's sleep.

The next morning, I found myself on Ragweed Valley Road, about nine miles outside of town. Ragweed Valley starts with a Baptist church on the corner, followed by a graveyard. Then you see the horse farms and chicken farms, and if you blink, you'll miss David's golf oasis. As I drove by it, I said, "That can't be it. That looks like a private club." Sure enough, it was a private club. His private club! David had some financial success with the release of his VHS tapes and book and decided to invest his money in his home and school. He bought sixty-four acres and turned it into a golfer's practice paradise.

As I approached the front door, I was greeted by none other than David Lee, a silver-haired gentleman who stood about 5-feet-10 and was in pretty good shape for a man in his mid-fifties. He had a slow southern drawl that might have put you to sleep, if not for the intriguing things he had to say. David had spared no expense when building his facility. The main clubhouse had a huge indoor putting area, good for about 25-footers on a carpet and running about a 10 on the stimp meter. Down a small hall were the doors for the men's and women's locker rooms. The rooms contained full tile showers, separate sinks and toilets and around twelve lockers, all oak with gold accents. Past the locker room was the workout and pool room. This room was surrounded by floor-to-ceiling mirrors and held a small custom-made swimming pool. Bean-shaped and maybe five feet deep, the pool was a small oasis during the hot Arkansas summers. A separate door in the back led to the sauna, and next to that was the massage room. There was a full Bowflex-type machine with all kinds of novelty workout gear. This place was amazing, and I hadn't even seen the grounds yet.

After David showed me around the clubhouse, we hopped into a golf cart from his private fleet and took a tour of the property. He began by showing me the range—two tiers looking over the property, each one about half the size of a football field. The range went just over 300 yards before narrowing and ending up at the other side on what David called the pro tee. I asked David if the grass down here was always so nice. It was like Augusta National in April. He told me that he was working with the University of Georgia on a new grass study to see if this type of Bermuda would grow this far north. The study certainly appeared to be a success based on the conditioning.

Beyond the range lay the three-hole course David designed. It started with a par-5 that stretched about 540 yards. It was a very demanding tee shot, which went through a chute of trees with a slight dogleg right. The greens were small and Bermuda, and hadn't been rolled in quite some time but certainly showed promise. The next hole was a good par-3, slightly downhill about 190 yards, followed by one of the toughest par-4 I had seen. Measuring 440 yards from the back, it was a slight dogleg right and had some very tall grass on both sides of the fairway. The second shot was an approach that one could only consider terrifying. The crowned postage stamp green sat on a rise about fifteen feet above a small pond, which guarded the front right. On the back was a farmer's fence with horses grazing in the distance. The fence was O.B., of course, mostly because it was electric to keep the horses in.

Heading back to the clubhouse, we drove over to the pro tee, an area about 100 feet long by 30 feet wide—basically a big flat rectangle of a perfectly manicured tee box, similar in condition to Augusta National. David's vision, so he explained, was for this area to be utilized by tour players when they came for lessons. At the time, it was used as a giant putting green for his golf schools, so students could practice extremely long lag putts. Adjacent to the clubhouse was a cabin-type structure that David nicknamed the "bunk house" for his tour program—a

program he was developing to find incredible athletes, who would be trained to compete on the pro tour in two years' time. In front of this six-bedroom cabin was a long, narrow putting green fronted by a pond. On the opposite side of the range was a sand bunker and another small chipping and putting green. This was truly an amazing place, and I was about to attend a golf school here.

Martha, the second student, arrived shortly after I did. School was now in session. David took us to the range and sat us in two big wicker chairs, while he explained his theory along with a brief history of golf. He demonstrated some shots and an hour later had us hit a few. He started us right out with some one-handed drills. I hit my first shots as pure as could be, with David quietly observing. After about five minutes, he asked if this was my first time practicing these drills. I told David that I had been working diligently on his drills for the past year or so. He said my swing looked really good but that I was faking the drills. Surprised by his bold statement and confused—what lead him to believe I was "faking the drills?" I looked at David, waiting for him to elaborate. I was here to learn and was open to whatever he had to say and teach. He explained that in a normal address position (with two feet on the ground and two hands holding the club), the golf swing movements are easy to fake because the body is in a position of strength, much like training wheels on a bicycle give you the false sense of balance. Exercises such as one-handed swings are more difficult to master and lead to the use of proper mechanics. David then instructed me to stand solely on my front left foot and with only my right hand on the club. He told me to lift the club over my head, not place it behind the ball, as I had learned in the book. He said that this would be the last step in removing the final "training wheel." This new drill was certainly more difficult and I immediately started struggling. My body needed a whole new set of movements to perform this action. It was now clear that I was truly "faking it" with my previous method.

After this exhaustive practice session (both in mind and body), David decided we'd had enough and it was time for lunch. He took us to Burl's Smokehouse about three miles away. Burl was a retired school superintendent who built the smokehouse and sold Indian and local artifacts. Burl was great friends with David and greeted us with a big smile and a warm welcome. The whole place made me feel at home. We had roast turkey sandwiches with homemade bread and baby Swiss cheese, a favorite of David's. During lunch, while Martha was looking around the country store, I approached David with my real reason for being there. I explained that I was not really there for a school, but to try to convince him to let me live full time at his facility and train to become a pro golfer on the PGA Tour. In a hesitant tone, he told me he would need to discuss it with his wife and would have a decision at the conclusion of the school tomorrow.

That night all I could think about was how amazing the facility was and how lucky I would be if he said yes. The next morning when I awoke, a strange feeling came over me. I remember feeling very alive and alert to what was really going on. I was in the middle of Arkansas, asking a golf pro to let me come and live near his home and train to be a tour pro. I started to get very emotional. Was this what I wanted? Why was I doing this? I had never shown that much interest in golf. As I sat contemplating these questions, I noticed a news story on the TV across the room. They were discussing a young man who was severely disfigured and limited in mobility, but he pushed on to play high school football. The story put my situation into perspective. I was lucky, and if this was what life had in store for me, then I should take full advantage of it. By the time I left that morning for David's place, I already knew I was going to be living there. The golf gods had already decided it. And they were smiling upon me.

Sure enough, at the conclusion of the day's school, David asked me to stay and chat. I said my goodbyes to Martha and

then headed into David's office to discuss my future. David started by asking what my plans for tomorrow were. I told him I was planning on driving to South Carolina to play some golf with my father, because I still had four days before I had to return to my job as a touring Broadway prop master. He told me that Golf magazine was coming to do a full story and photo shoot about his facility and that he was planning on using one of his head instructors to be the model for the swing photos. He proceeded to tell me that I had one of the best looking swings he had ever seen. If I canceled my trip and agreed to be the swing model for the photos, he said, I could come back in two months to live there full time and train. David would not charge me for training. Instead, I would work for him in the mornings until noon, five days a week, and then the rest of the day would be mine to train my swing. I eagerly accepted this offer and couldn't wait to call home to tell everyone the news! Not only was I getting my wish to train with David Lee, but I was going to be in the January 1999 issue of Golf magazine. I was in total shock and so was my family. I don't think they expected all this to happen, but they gave their full support to what I was doing.

The following day was clear and sunny, perfect for a photo shoot. We met the photographer and the woman writing the article on David and his methods. David explained to her that I was a very talented player who he was going to turn into a tour pro. He had me demonstrate a few swings before they turned on the camera. David told me to hit some no-reference drivers, which essentially meant I should not put the club behind the ball at address. Instead, I should start with the club upright in the same position as the top of my backswing.

"I don't want to give your brain a chance to cheat," he said. "If I let you place the club behind the ball, you can use your proprioception to cheat the drill. By starting this way, you are forcing the brain to figure out a way that is not so eye-hand coordinated."

I immediately tensed up. I had never used a driver with this drill and now I had someone filming and watching me. I was a nervous wreck. The first three shots were cold whiffs; the next two were hit so poorly I felt bad for the poor ball. David suddenly told me to stop. He put his hand around my shoulder and we walked a few feet away so no one else could hear. Then, just like the horse whisperer, he said, "Are you nervous?"

"Yes I'm nervous! There is a camera filming and all this pressure to perform."

"OK. Well, pressure is to be expected in this type of situation, and you will be facing plenty of it when you play professionally, so we need to prepare you. Here is what I want you to do: On the next swing, I want you to get more aggressive with your shoulder turn. Speed the whole thing up. Jack Nicklaus taught me this. He swings the hardest on the tightest holes. It gets all the tension out of his arms so he can let it go instead of steering it, which never works."

With this understanding in mind, I went back to hit again and sure enough … bam! I smacked it perfect right down the middle. I continued to hit shot after shot solid and straight. The woman doing the article was shocked. She turned to David and curiously asked "What did you tell him?!" With a coy smile and his signature slow southern drawl, David said, "That's a secret you only get when you come to one of my schools." Everyone laughed, of course, as David had a real way with people, and he truly loved teaching golf.

We spent the next few hours talking and hitting shots for the camera. By the end of the day, I was utterly exhausted yet thrilled at the same time. I thanked David for the opportunity and assured him I would be back in two months to start my training.

CHAPTER 4

Many of life's failures are people who did not realize how close they were to success when they gave up
– Thomas Edison

WHEN I ARRIVED back home and told my family and friends what happened, they were ecstatic for me and in a state of disbelief. I could hardly believe it myself, but it was happening. My first course of action was to tell my boss I would be leaving the theater to pursue my golf career. Surprisingly, that was easier and went better than expected. He wished me luck, and off I went to Arkansas. My family was very supportive, but my father was a little skeptical about David's claim that he could train me in eighteen months for the pro tour. But he gave me his blessing, nonetheless, and wished me good luck.

With only my golf clubs and some essential clothes, I got in my 93 Honda Civic and made the twenty-hour journey to Arkansas on February 1, 1999. Needless to say, I was exhausted when I finally arrived. I decided to stay in a little local hotel until I found a more permanent place next to the Gravity Golf facility. I didn't have Internet, so the process of finding lodging facilities meant scouring the local papers and asking townspeople for advice. Three days into my search, I discovered a perfect little lake cabin, right on Lake Hamilton.

It was very private and had everything I needed—the necessities of a bed, stove, fridge and a bathroom with a hot shower. With no frills and only 130 square feet, it was definitely what some might consider "roughing it," but I was there to train, not stay indoors.

My first day at Gravity Golf turned out to be a tutorial for how to answer the phone and take orders for books and schools. For four hours each day, from 8 a.m. to noon, I would be booking golf schools and answering people's golf questions. The rest of the day was mine to train and play golf. My first lesson in old-school charm came from David's wife, Cricket. My New York aggressive phone mannerisms were a bit too brash for her liking, and she eventually taught me how to be a southern gentleman. My golf training also began that same day. David came out onto the tee, sat in a chair and watched me hitting balls. He gave me a couple drills and discussed some expectations he had for me. It was a bitter February day and quite windy, so after about twenty minutes, David wished me good luck and said he would see me inside later. He was a man of few words with a contemplative nature and dry sense of humor. I stayed outside for three more hours and hit over 500 balls. I came inside frozen but not deterred at all.

This process went on each day with David varying the drills but not really spending that much time with me on the range. One day he gave me a 2 iron and said, "When you can hit this with a perfect draw in these drills, then we might have something." I spent the next three months with that 2 iron and no draw. I had a wicked slice and it seemed like it wasn't getting any better. When I first arrived at Gravity Golf, I had asked David when he thought my slice would disappear. I recall him saying in about three months. Well, three months came and went, but my slice was still there. Truth be told, it was nearly gone, but I was a perfectionist who wanted to see perfect results. That was when David told me something

very important. He called it the gravity syndrome. It's when someone expects to hit the ball perfect every time because they can do it on the range. He felt that this expectation was not realistic. His message to me was this: Realize that what's important is to have good misses, shots that you could recover from instead of being out of bounds.

I started noticing an improvement in my game, but after ten months, I was nowhere near being a scratch golfer. I remember breaking 80 with a 79 and thinking how difficult it has been to get that point. Shooting a 69 seemed a world away. It was around this time that I started getting worried that the one-year plan might not be realistic. I had only saved enough money to get me through a full year of training, yet ten months had already gone by. My initial thought was that if I could be fully trained after twelve months and then acquire sponsors, my money worries would be over. The reality was, I needed more money now or this dream was going to be just that … a dream. As I was sitting in the clubhouse stressing about money and how to save my golf career, the phone rang. On the line was an eager gentleman inquiring about the infomercial he saw on TV. He wanted to book a school with David Lee. I was accustomed to taking calls like this and immediately said, "OK, let me see what's available. When would you like to come?" The gentleman gave me his dates, and I explained to him that unfortunately David was all booked during that time period, as were the other teachers. I told him I would keep his info and if anyone canceled, I would let him know right away. It was at that moment, right after hanging up the phone, that I saw the solution to my financial problems.

I walked straight into David's office and explained to him that during the past several months, I had turned away over thirty students interested in booking schools. The reason being that Gravity Golf had only three teachers; and they were all in different states. Instead of turning away all these students and money, maybe I could start teaching. It would further my development and understanding of the game, not to mention that the pressure of performing in front of students would be an added confidence-builder and preparation for tournament golf. And money—let's not forget about money. Teaching would allow me to make important contacts. And contacts meant sponsors and money.

I told David my idea, and then looked at him, waiting for a response. After what seemed like forever, he pointedly said to me, "You want to teach? OK. Sounds good to me. I'll give you 25 percent of the schools you teach and the rest goes to Gravity Golf." And just like that my teaching career began.

CHAPTER
5

You cannot teach a man anything, you can only help him find it within himself
– Galileo Galiiei

My first golf school came and went, and before I knew it, I was brimming with confidence and making enough money to allow myself another year of training. Teaching a school was a great confidence-booster for my self-esteem. Previously, most of my days were spent alone on the range, hitting what I felt weren't the greatest golf shots. Now, when I would teach a school and demonstrate my swing, people would sit in awe. I had their full attention and I loved it. Many of these students had arrived at Gravity Golf as a last resort. They had been to a slew of other instructors at various schools, just as I had, searching for direction and a clear understanding of the game of golf, only to be disappointed. For most of these students, money was no object. All they wanted was a method to help their game. Gravity Golf gave these students something they had never experienced before—a totally new approach, one that challenged them physically and mentally. And watching me hit perfect one-handed and one-footed shots made them believers in no time. I was regularly getting offers from students to financially back me for tournament play, but in my heart I knew I was nowhere near a tour-level player. By this time, I could shoot in the high 70s and my swing looked great to the naked eye, but the truth was, I had a long way to go.

I became relentless in my practice, and anyone driving by the facility could bear witness to me hitting thousands of balls day after day. One day, a gentleman by the name of Melvin Wallace stopped by. He was a retired drama teacher from a small college in Texas and now lived only five miles from Gravity Golf on the picturesque Lake Ouachita.

"Well hello there young man," he said to me. "I have driven by this facility so many times and couldn't help but notice all the practicing going on. I just had to stop by and see what this was all about." I proceeded to explain Gravity Golf to Melvin and within minutes, he asked me for a few private lessons, which I gladly accepted. With that, my friendship with Melvin Wallace began. He was a terrible golfer and had all the characteristics of a poor swing. He would fidget over the ball, was too deliberate with all his actions, and expected perfect results. Beyond that, he was probably one of the most personable, generous men I had ever met. He was always supportive of my development and was intent on improving his own game, too.

During one of our lessons, Melvin asked me if I would like to play golf as his guest at Hot Springs Village, where he was a member. I had been hearing about Hot Springs Village for quite some time but never had an offer to play out there. Hot Springs Village is one of the largest gated private communities in the United States, with a population of about 20,000 people. It includes a total of nine world-renown golf courses, five of which are ranked annually as the best in the state. To play golf at Hot Springs Village, you have to be a member or play as a guest of a member. And the only way to become a member is to own a piece of property within the Village. Without hesitation, I graciously accepted Melvin's invitation. He told me that he had a couple of golfing brothers,

John and Mark Rose, who lived in the Village and would be joining us.

Melvin and I decided to meet at the course. When I arrived at the front gate, I received a pass and directions to the course. We would be playing the Ponce De Leon course, 6,900 yards carved through a rolling forest. Lakes, streams, and perfect white sand bunkers were everywhere. The fee for members was only $18, but for guests, it was $60. Melvin had a couple guest passes that allowed me to pay the member fee, which was a huge help.

Melvin introduced me to Johnny and Mark. Mark was about ten years my senior, and his hand nearly swallowed mine when he shook it. He was a normal-size guy around six feet tall, but his hands were huge! I later found out that Mark had been a wide receiver for the University of Arkansas when Lou Holtz was the coach. It's pretty hard to drop passess when you have hands that big. Mark suffered a really bad shoulder injury during a game, ending his career, but you could see he was still as strong as an ox. Johnny was an athlete as well, but not for the past few years. Instead, he had taken to burgers and beer. Portly would be the word to best describe Johnny. Both guys where true southern gentlemen and made me feel very accepted right away. The round was a blast. Johnny and Mark were both solid players and could both break 80. I don't remember the final scores, but I do remember exchanging phone numbers with Johnny and telling all three of them how much fun I had. Little did I know at the time that Johnny would end up becoming one of my best friends.

A few weeks passed before Melvin came by Gravity Golf for one of his lessons. At that time, he presented me with an enticing proposition: "How would you like to buy some land up in Hot Springs Village so you can become a member and play golf all the time?" My eyes lit up. There was only one problem: I was nearly broke and the little money I did make went to my housing and training.

Melvin continued, "It's a really great deal, and you need to practice at a full length course, not just at a range with three practice holes." I knew he was right; anyone serious about playing needed to be on really fast greens and needed a variety of terrain. With nine courses, Hot Springs Village offered all of this. It all came back to money, though, and I just didn't have it. Reluctantly, I had to decline Melvin's offer. "But I haven't even told you the price yet," he said. "Well unless it's the cheapest land in America, I don't think I'll be joining anytime soon," I responded with a smile. Melvin told me that he would be back in a few days with the deed, and if I couldn't afford the property at that time, it was no problem.

Sure enough, a few days later, Mel returned with the deed, telling me to take a look. The deed said the property was purchased in 1976 for $5,000. I could only imagine what it was now in 2001. Melvin explained that his friend bought a whole bunch of these lots back in the 1970s in the hope of a huge boom in the housing market in the Hot Springs Village area. Unfortunately, that wasn't the case. When it didn't pan out, Melvin's friend was left paying the taxes and yearly dues for the club. It was only about $20 for the taxes and $30 for the monthly dues—not bad if you only have one lot, but he had a couple dozen. This was simply too much of a burden for him. Melvin went on to say that his friend was willing to sell me one lot for a lump sum of $400. "You're telling me that $400 is all it'll take? It's a deal!" I signed the paperwork right there, and for the first time in my life, I owned a piece of land. I couldn't wait to get up to the Village and see my lot. I thanked Melvin profusely for his generosity and the help with my golf career. He told me it was an honor to help a nice young man like myself, even if I was a Yankee from New York! Almost everyone I met in the South loved to bust my chops about being from New York, but in the end, they always treated me with respect and courtesy.

The next week, after the rest of the paperwork was sorted

out, I reached out to Johnny Rose to see if he wanted to play a round of golf with a new member. He said of course, and from that day on, Johnny and I became golf buddies and the best of friends. He showed me around the Village and we played all of the courses countless times. By the end of my first year in Arkansas, I had shot par once—not the tour scores I was hoping for but good enough to convince myself that I needed to stay and commit more time to my game.

David felt my progress was slowed because of my inability to throw a baseball with any velocity. His theory was that the golf swing, at its highest level, was equal to that of a baseball pitcher throwing a fastball at 90 mph. And in his eyes, I didn't have the mechanics, given that my velocity only reached 50 mph. I became even more obsessed about figuring this game out. David felt that the lack of velocity and poor throwing motion would take care of itself if I continued working on the one-handed drills. I had no problem with this rationale, as I truly loved working on all the drills. Where most people rush to play on the course, I thoroughly enjoyed endless hours of practice. I was honing my skill, and every swing got me closer to what I thought were perfect mechanics. I was able to feel, through all the drills, just how sensitive this mechanism of the golf swing really was. In a normal swing with both hands and feet in their normal positions, things became cloudy and all subtly was lost. I lived in the drills, and anytime I would deviate from them, David would be there to steer me back in the right direction. His guidance was instrumental in teaching me about perseverance.

CHAPTER 6

Creativity takes courage
– Henri Matisse

AFTER ABOUT A YEAR and a half, I was still shooting in the 70s and 80s. Seeing how frustrated I was, David tried to keep me motivated by giving me constant encouragement and presenting new theories as to why my development was not accelerating. But I really think he just knew it would take time—no other way around it. Finally, one day on the course with Johnny, I had a breakthrough. It wasn't a swing thought or anything like that. It was just a great round. I shot a 66 out of nowhere and had no idea how I did it. As soon as I got off the course, I called David to tell him the good news. "I told you it would happen!" David said excitingly. "Now it's time to start playing some tournaments to see how it holds up under pressure." This was my first round in the 60s and my coach was already pushing me to play in tournaments! My confidence in my game didn't match David's, but he reassured me that this was all part of the process. So with a leap of faith, I signed up to play in a Monday qualifier for the Nike Tour.

The tournament was being held about 70 miles north of Hot Springs in a small town called Fort Smith. Before I left

Gravity Golf that morning, David gave me his view on how I should play the round. He said to play from an up-route mode, which meant I would not be addressing the ball with the clubhead behind the ball, but instead I would walk into the shot with the club straight up and down. Then when I felt ready, I would turn my shoulders back and the club would be ready to fall into the perfect downswing position. David's thinking was that by doing this, I would be making a swing that had no backswing, which meant fewer moving (body) parts to coordinate. With fewer moving parts, my swing was more likely to hold up under pressure than if it had more moving parts. This seemed to make sense, so I was willing to take a chance. Upon arriving at the tournament, my nerves started to kick in. This was my first professional tournament and I didn't feel I was ready. The next thing I knew, I was in the bathroom getting sick. I kept thinking, What the hell am I doing here? I can't break 80 on most days, and now I'm teeing it up with 100 golfers, all vying for a spot on the Nike Tour.

I finally made it to the first tee, and when they announced my name I was shaking and my heart was pounding out of my chest. I stood up to the ball, raised the club over my head, and took a vicious rip at it. Bam! I smacked it right into the pond about thirty yards in front of the tee. I was mortified and the swing felt terrible. I finally got off the first tee, and I stuck with the up-route position for the first nine holes, which I finished at 8-over par. I was so embarrassed that on the tenth tee, I switched back to my normal golf swing. I made three birdies on the back and finished with a score of 96. It was not the round I was hoping for, but I felt a real sense of accomplishment. I was living out my dream of playing professional golf.

When I arrived back at Gravity Golf, I was a little dejected for not playing better, but David was there to put things in perspective, "Noah, only a year and a half ago you couldn't hit shots without a slice. Now, you are shaping shots and competing against golfers who have been playing tournament golf for years." I knew he was right, but coming in near dead last in the competition stung just a little.

Soon enough I was right back to practicing and teaching full time. I was committed to improving my game and seeing this thing through. David began making the drills more difficult for me. He put me in what he called his "3-hop drill." This drill consisted of me standing about five or six feet behind the ball, taking my swing to the top of the backswing, holding that position, and then hopping only on my front left leg until I was in the right position to strike the ball, never letting my back foot touch the ground. This drill was a beast. It took me several times just to make solid contact with the ball. Once I was hitting it well, my body could only sustain doing maybe six or seven more attempts before I was totally exhausted. The drill built up my stamina and coordination. It also was a huge help in learning about balance. I was starting to get a pretty solid foundation under which to swing the golf club. I could feel that maybe it was time to start taking my physical conditioning to a new level, as well as my diet.

David would have all kinds of athletes and pro golfers come through Gravity Golf, and one such student was Gabrielle Reece, the renowned Olympic volleyball player. She chose David and Gravity Golf because she felt that with some proper training maybe she could make it on the LPGA Tour. She and I became quick friends, often hitting balls together on the range. Gabrielle introduced me to a workout program she recently discovered called ProBodX.

ProBodX was designed by Marv Marinovich and Edythe M. Heus, D.C. Marv was one of the first ever strength and conditioning coaches hired in the NFL. After leaving the NFL, he invented his own style of teaching and training. Marv's basic theory as far as I could tell was that the human body has over 400 muscles and if your workout doesn't work all

of them, some muscles develop and others don't, leaving you open to injury. The workout consisted of very light weights but plenty of balance exercises performed on a balance ball. I fell in love with this workout and adopted it as part of my daily routine. I was building lean, fast-twitch muscles. ProBodX helped me in my golf game—in no time at all my ball speed, my posture and my stamina were all improving.

My teaching was also really taking off around this time. My students were very receptive to my teaching approach, and as word spread, a week didn't go by that my lesson book wasn't full of students. I believed wholeheartedly in Gravity Golf and was so passionate about it that my students and David himself nominated me for Golf Digest's Top Teachers in America. Much to my delight, I won this distinguished award and then a short time later, was also nominated for Golf Magazine's Top Teachers list. As reaffirming as these accolades were, my main focus was still on playing golf, not teaching golf.

My daily schedule consisted of waking up early each morning and training before my students arrived. I would get to the range before sun-up and line up golf balls on the ground. I lined up 100 balls in a row, about four inches apart, and did this seven more times for a total of 1,400 golf balls. I then began hitting balls from all the different drills David taught me. It would take me two or three hours to hit all the balls, and I would do this, on average, about three or four days a week, with shorter sessions on the remaining days, leaving time and energy to play some golf as well. I don't think I could have ever survived this grueling schedule without the ProBodX workout. My body was becoming a finely tuned instrument, and my golf game was beginning to show some real changes as well. One day, while playing the three holes on David's property with his son Danny, I made a hole-in-one on the par-3, which measured 190 yards. I couldn't believe it! All this hard work was showing some real results. My teaching was also improving, because the more I practiced, the more intimate I became with Gravity Golf and its philosophy. After about six months of this training schedule, I decided it was time for another tournament.

Feeling confident and ready, I signed up for the New England Golf Tour in Springfield, Massachusetts, and booked my plane ticket. My parents decided to join me on the trip, as did my friend Jeff Jordan, a tour player who also trained with David Lee. I would play in two tournaments (only 30 miles apart), each 36 holes and both in the same week. My father agreed to be my caddie, which, in retrospect, was not the best idea. The never-ending desire to prove myself to my father turned out to be far too much pressure for me at this early stage of my development.

CHAPTER 7

If you do not expect the unexpected you will not find it, for it is not to be reached by search or trail
– Heraclitus

I ARRIVED AT THE COURSE early that morning to warm up before the round. At this point in my training, my swing was very erratic. I could shoot 69 to 89 in a heartbeat. This inconsistency made me incredibly nervous, so I spent hours before any tournament warming up, hoping to hone my game before tee-off.

The first tournament was a disaster, with my father and me butting heads the whole time. Being a perfectionist, I expected my caddie to obey all the rules and take a serious, thoughtful approach. My father, on the other hand, made light of his caddie duties and displayed more of an apathetic attitude. This irritated me to no end. At one point, I even told him that the job of a good caddie was to "show up, shut up, and hurry up!" My father found this hysterical. I did not. I wasn't playing some small tournament; this was the big time. And my father was making a joke of it. I was mentally questioning everything he did, which prevented me from focusing on the game. I shot an 82, and all hopes of winning the tournament were over.

The next day when I arrived on the course, the head official for the tournament informed me that anyone who shot 10 shots over the leader the day before would be eligible for a separate event. It was a one-day shootout for low score, and the cost was $40. I got in the shootout only after my father said he would pay. I felt I had no chance at all, but my father had seen enough to feel maybe I did. Sure enough, after warming up for my normal two hours, I went out and shot a 75, which turned out to be the low score. Now 75 might not seem that great to some, but for me it was the first money I had ever won against anyone who considered himself a pro. I was ecstatic. I felt as though maybe I would be ready to compete for some real money in the next tournament, which was only in two days' time and happened to be just a few miles away from Springfield.

So there I was at my second tournament, feeling excited and ready to play—a welcome change from the nerve-shattering first tournament. I would be teeing off in the last group of the day. One of the competitors in my threesome dropped out at the last minute, which meant I would be playing with just one other player. I can't recall his name, but I do remember his game. On the very first hole, I started out great with a nice par. It probably would have been a birdie, but the greens had been aerated only a few days earlier and were beyond bumpy. I took it in stride and realized everyone would have the same disadvantage. My playing partner did not see it the same way. After he missed his putt and tapped in, he started cursing and threw his club about 20 yards in the direction of his bag.

Now I had my moments of frustration on the golf course, but I never lost my cool like this guy. Every time he made a bad swing, he went off in a tirade, throwing clubs, cursing and making the whole situation very uncomfortable. One aspect of the game I have always liked is that golf, unlike most other sports, is a gentleman's game, so I always tried to act like one. I prided myself at being the best dressed anytime

I represented the game, and I always followed the rules, no matter how ridiculous I thought they might be. I would often joke that I was the consummate pro-fashional player even if I didn't play well.

By the time we got to the sixth hole, my playing partner was in rare form. As he stood over his chip shot off the edge of the green, he once again duffed his shot. He threw the club across the green, screaming about the condition of the course. After we putted out, he came up to me, shook my hand and said, "I'm done. I think I have the flu and can't play anymore." He took his bag and walked off. That left me with no playing partner. Dad and I both started laughing and shrugged our shoulders. I couldn't play on my own because someone besides me needed to keep my score. Teeing off last meant there were no other competitors on the course to pair up with. Just then, the tournament director pulled up in his golf cart, so I explained the situation. He had a solution to my problem; he would be my playing partner and, in turn, could keep my score. Up until this point, I was even par and playing pretty solid despite the crazy, erratic partner.

When we started playing again, I felt really relaxed with the tournament director. I was now playing with someone who was not competing with me, so I felt much less stress. The fact was, I was still in a competition; it just didn't feel like it. I started out on the next hole making a great birdie, and for the first time on this whole trip, I was in red numbers. My dad started cheering me on and before I knew it, I was 2-under after nine holes. By the time I reached the seventh hole, a long par-5, I was still 2-under, and with a ten-foot uphill birdie putt, I could see this round being my first in the 60s during a tournament. My father and I read the putt, which amusingly resembled a Plinko board with all the aeration holes. I took dead aim and nailed the putt dead center. I finished with a par on eighteen and a 69 for the round. As we walked off the green, the tournament director said, "Great job! I bet that's the low score for the day. Those greens were brutal." I was shocked; I had never thought I would be in the lead.

When we went into the scoring tent, I discovered I was in a tie for second place, just behind one other gentleman, who had shot a 66. I would be in the final group the next day. Needless to say, that night I was beyond excited. My parents and I, along with Jeff, who shot an impressive 71, went to dinner and celebrated. It was a truly great feeling.

The next day I was introduced to my new playing partners, Eric Eagle and Mark Maddish, both seasoned veterans at tournament golf. Eric had Monday-qualified for the PGA Tour three times and was in New England preparing for Q-School (a grueling qualifying tournament for the PGA Tour). On the first hole, I saw why he and Mark were at the top of the tournament. They both drove the ball about thirty yards farther than I did and were simply at a higher playing level than me at that point. I held my own, but while they were continuously making birdies, I was scrambling for pars. The day finished with me shooting a 75, tied with my friend Jeff for sixth place. Jeff had a great second round, and the fact we tied made for some great conversation on the way back to Arkansas. The highlight of the trip was receiving my first check as a professional. It was for a whopping $400, which to me might as well have been a million. By accepting this money, I was now officially a pro golfer and had given up my amateur status. In retrospect, this was one decision I ended up regretting. I was not ready to be a pro. Spending a couple more years playing amateur events, honing my craft, probably would have been more beneficial to my growth as a competitor.

CHAPTER 8

Either I will find a way, or I will make one
– Philip Sidney

When I returned to Arkansas this time around, there was no letdown in my game; I was starting to see the results I had always hoped for. Pushing myself to the limit with each practice session was just what I needed. My mentality was this: The more difficult the drills and the quicker I could master them, the quicker I would improve my game and move to the next level. I began doing the toughest drills that David created and started experimenting with some of my own, including the no-look drill. I discovered this drill when I was in the sand bunker at the Isabella Golf Course in Hot Springs Village. It was one of those days when I was having a really hard time hitting sand shots. Some were thin, some were fat. I was all over the map. Out of frustration, I just took a full rip out of the sand. Only this time, I wasn't trying to hit the ball; I was just letting go of some frustration. I kept my focus on the flagstick and took a swing.

When your focus is on the flagstick and not on the ball, you can't take a full backswing because your spine is already in a twisted position. A shorter backswing isn't a big deal with a shot of this length. So when I struck the ball, it came out of the sand in a way that I had never felt or seen. It was perfect with just the right amount of spin. I was in shock. I kept hitting this shot over and over with the same result. When I put my head back in the normal position (focusing on the ball, not the flagstick), I would hit it poorly again. What was going on? I worked on this type of swing for a few weeks, even trying to hit drivers in this same manner. The distance was terribly limited, but the contact was to die for. I realized that the eyes must have some hold on the swing, which was causing me to flex and strike at the ball on the downswing, rather than swing through the ball as I did in the drill. When the eyes or brain could not see the ball, all instinct to strike at the ball was gone. My only problem was, as soon as I looked back at the ball, I lashed at it again. I was determined to find a way to have the best of both worlds: look at the ball and have no lash or strike.

I came up with the idea to take an old pair of sunglasses and cover the lenses with duct tape. I addressed the ball with my normal stance and head position. I then looked through the bottom of the glasses and peeked at the ball. When I was ready to swing, I tilted my head into its normal position so the glasses blocked my view of impact. Taking a "normal" swing, I was never able to see the ball or the impact. This worked perfectly, having the same effect as turning my head, except now I wasn't limited with my spine and backswing rotation. You might ask why I didn't just close my eyes during the swing. The reason was balance. When your eyes are closed, your balance becomes compromised. With the glasses on, I could still see peripherally, just not the ball and impact. From then on, I incorporated this into my training. It helped me learn how to stop flexing at the moment of impact. In essence, you should feel as if the fastest point in the swing is at impact or beyond, not before it. Even if my reasoning was wrong, the feel and action of the ball was right, and to me, that was

all that mattered.

Months went by and I continued my drills, played a ton of golf, and kept my health and diet at peak form. But it seemed I had reached a plateau. My game was at a standstill. I was very frustrated because all I wanted was to play on tour and compete against top pros. It had now been four long years of solid training and teaching. I had yet to shoot lower than a 66. And even with a score like that, I couldn't maintain that level of play on a daily basis. My goal at the start of this endeavor was not just to become a scratch golfer. I wanted to be on tour with the best in the world. As before, David had all kinds of theories as to why I was not improving. But I wanted real answers, not theories. My frustration boiled over into an argument one day with David asking me to leave Gravity Golf. I was halfway out the door when Cricket, in her usual rational manner, stopped me and calmed us both down. David and I apologized to each other and both agreed that it was frustrating not to see the expected results after so much time and effort had been invested.

Somewhere around that time, Melvin stopped by to chat with David, as they had become close friends. He told David about a young player he was introduced to named Ralph Raines. According to Mel, Ralph was an impressive player. I was a little skeptical because poor golfers have a way of hyping up decent players. But this turned out not to be the case. Ralph was one hell of a good golfer. David gave one of our instructional DVDs to Mel, asking him to invite Ralph to come down and work with us. A year earlier, David had made a DVD collection that showed me doing all the drills with him explaining why they were used. I gave my testimonial and my personal story with Gravity Golf.

About a month passed before Ralph stopped by Gravity Golf. I arrived to find David giving him a lesson on the tee. Ralph immediately introduced himself to me and said I was one of the main reasons he decided to come here. He had watched the DVDs and said seeing my swing and hearing how passionate I was about Gravity Golf was all the convincing he needed. David and I worked with Ralph all day on his game, sharing with him all we could. By the end of the day, Ralph decided this was the right direction for him and made a commitment to come to the Gravity Golf facility as often as he could. He lived about 70 miles away in Rixby, Arkansas, so a daily commute was a tough task, but he was committed to improving.

Ralph and I became quick friends. He told me just how hard it was on all the mini tours. He was playing a pretty full schedule and not having that much success. This was a real letdown for me, because Ralph regularly outperformed me on the course yet he could not do the drills anywhere near the level that I could. I began to question if all the drill work was really helping my full swing.

Ralph told me how all the top players were using video to analyze their swings, which David wasn't really into. In our free time, Ralph and I began using video to try to see if we could make any improvements. We spent the next full year doing drills, playing golf and trying to analyze the swing. Each time we thought we had found something that produced tangible results, we would find that in a week or in a matter of days, this discovery no longer worked. This was the most frustrating thing I had ever been a part of. At least with Gravity Golf, I had someone to blame for not improving; this was all on me. I was beginning to see why golf was considered the most difficult activity to master and why only a few hundred people had ever made a real living at it. Ralph had some minor success on the mini tours, but when it came to playing with the big boys, we were both outclassed. At this point, I was nearing five years at Gravity Golf without much professional tournament success other than the New England series. Ralph and I decided that it was time to try a PGA Tour Monday qualifier. We signed up for one down in Dallas, Tex-

as. I was still behind Ralph in ability, but I felt I needed to push myself to see if I was improving.

We arrived at the tournament without a solid foundation or understanding of the swing. I had so many ideas about what a proper swing was; I was definitely overthinking. The day proved to be a struggle, to say the least. I plunked two balls in the water on the eighteenth hole to finish the round 9-over par. I choked really bad, and Ralph didn't fare much better.

I was reaching my wit's end, so when my father called to see how I did, I assured him it was terrible. "Well you gave it one hell of a try, Noah. I'm very proud of you for making it this far. Maybe you need a break from golf for a while. I have a new show going on the road—would you like to take a year off from golf and join the tour?" I said yes without hesitation. I saw no future with Gravity Golf other than teaching, and seeing that I was not reaching the levels of success I had hoped for, I was not committed to the teaching. My heart just wasn't into it at this point.

Ralph and I decided to head to dinner and discuss his future as well. We ended up at the hotel restaurant, had a few cocktails, and reminisced about the round and our friendship. We drove back to Arkansas the next day, as I would be packing up and heading to Chicago at the end of the week to join the "The Color Purple" tour. When I told David of my plans, he was, of course, disappointed and felt that I was very close to figuring it all out. But that's just it: It always seemed I was "very close" but never quite there. It was time for me to step away for a bit and clear my head. David wished me well, and with a handshake and a hug, I said goodbye.

CHAPTER 9

The only freedom is the freedom from the known
– Jiddu Krishnamurti

AFTER SAYING GOODBYE to David and Cricket, I decided to head to the Village and play one last round of golf before the long ride to Chicago. There was no one else I would rather play with than my good friend Johnny Rose. This would be our last round for quite a while. We spoke for a bit about my future and how I'd miss Arkansas and then wished each other luck on this round. I addressed the ball on the 395-yard par-4. As I stood looking out at the fairway and thinking about how long I had been trying to perfect and master this game, I had a sudden insight. I had tried Gravity Golf, Hank Haney Golf, Mo Norman Golf. I had tried various types of swing theories, including my own creations, and still I was not able to compete at a tour level. In that moment, I asked myself a question that I had never asked before:

What would happen if I didn't approach the golf swing with an idea, belief or method guiding my swing?

This was such a profound question that I felt an explosion in my mind! My mind did not know how to approach such a

question or statement. My mind was responsible for researching all these different methodologies. What would happen if I put all that down? I stood on the tee, staring at the ball in a total state of awareness. I had no idea what would happen if I didn't consciously direct my swing, but I was about to find out. When I started back with the club, it didn't feel fast or slow; it was just an action not being guided by thought. Nothing in my body was leading or trailing. The golf club hit the ball with my body in a position I had never been in before. The ball left the club and headed right down the center of the fairway. Johnny was amazed, as was I. "Wow! Nice drive! Never saw you hit it that far on this hole before," said Johnny.

"I have never hit a ball like that in my life!" I exclaimed.

Something had happened; I felt a sense of tremendous space inside my mind. My mind was free of thought and ideas; therefore, I had no direction or guide, just pure freedom. I was allowing my mind to swing however it wanted without any sense of control. As I approached the next shot without fear of the outcome, I could feel this expansive state of mind once again. I was not sure what I would produce; I only knew that it would not be based on an idea or belief about how to swing. No scientific process and no mental effort. Just swinging without anything in mind. I would allow myself freedom from all beliefs about how to swing. My next shot hit the flagstick from 90 yards! I proceeded to hit a total of three flagsticks that day for the nine holes of golf we played. "Johnny, I think I might have just found something new today."

The next morning I was leaving Arkansas and heading north to Chicago to start my new job with "The Color Purple." On my way north, I decided to stop in Rixby, Arkansas, to see Ralph. I called him after my incredible round that day and told him that he needed to meet with me early in the morning to discuss what I had found. "So what is this idea that you have to tell me about?" asked Ralph. He was, of course, a little hesitant because we had been through all this before. The mind had given us thousands of ideas on how to swing the club, and all of them turned out to be dead ends. Ralph was just like me, always thinking about the swing but always with the same unsatisfying results. A few days of good golf was inevitably followed by disaster once whatever new technique we were trying wore off. I can honestly say I wasn't exactly sure if this was one of those discoveries or not. It just seemed so different and certainly I had never hit three flagsticks in nine holes before. So there I was, standing at this little rundown driving range in Arkansas that at 7 a.m. hadn't even opened yet for the day, about to share my discovery.

Ralph looked at me. "So what do you want me to do?"

"That's just it, Ralph. I don't want you to do anything," I began to explain.

"I want you to let go of all your ideas and beliefs about how to swing the club. I don't want you to use any effort from your mind or body. If your brain says turn your hips, don't. If your mind says stay on plane, don't. Just swing how fast or slow your brain decides, without any conscious control. Let your body move whenever it wants to, not when you tell it to."

Looking a bit confused, Ralph said he'd give it a try. "No! That's the opposite of what you should do. That's what we have been doing all these years—trying to swing a certain way. I want you not to try; I want you to be free from any kind of mental or physical control. I want you to give up all control and just see what the mind, free of thought, is able to produce," I explained to Ralph. Without hesitation, Ralph took a swing. The first shot was perfect, as was the second and all the remaining swings in that session.

Ralph and I would always video our practice sessions, and this time was no different. When we reviewed the film, we were stunned. We noticed no real deviation from our normal swings, but the results were drastically better. Why were our results so much better without our mechanics

changing? Unfortunately, I didn't have time to explore this more, because I was about to head to Chicago and wouldn't be able to practice for at least two more weeks. Ralph would have to be the guinea pig. He seemed as perplexed as I was about why this approach was working and assured me he would keep me posted on his progress.

CHAPTER
10

If one is a master of one thing and understands one thing well, one has at the same time, insight into and understanding of many things
– Vincent Van Gogh

OVER THE NEXT TWO WEEKS, some amazing things began to unfold. After only three days, an ecstatic Ralph called me and said he just shot a 65 on his home course and had been hitting one perfect shot after another on the range. I was so happy for him—the U.S. Open qualifier was only ten days away, and if Ralph was playing this well, he might just have a chance to make it. I would also be trying out for the U.S. Open on the same day as Ralph, but my qualifying would be in Chicago. My only problem was that due to my round-the-clock Broadway work schedule, I'd have no time at all to practice my game during the next ten days. Still, I was very curious to see how this new understanding would perform under the stressful conditions of tournament play.

As the ten days passed, Ralph kept calling and telling me how much better he was getting. I almost couldn't believe it because he was shooting mid to low 60s every day, which was something neither of us ever seemed able to do on a consistent basis. But here he was, doing it day after day. I, on the other

hand, was having a totally different experience. Being that I was unable to hit any golf balls because of my work schedule, I was curious to see if maybe I could apply my new understanding to other aspects of life. This first happened while I was having breakfast in a little diner in downtown Chicago, recalling the moment of my breakthrough only a few days earlier. I remembered standing over the golf ball, free from all thought about the swing. During that moment, free from all ideas and beliefs, I instantly became acutely aware of everything. My mind was alert in a way that it had never been before. I could see, feel, hear, and smell everything at once. I felt the tightness of my grip pressure. I could feel the worn-out spots on the grip where my hours of practice had worn it down. I was aware of every sensation in and around my body at once. I smelled the air with its subtly of freshly cut grass, and I could see the ball and the ground in a way I had never seen before. The ball was bright white, and each piece of grass was unique and alive. I was in a state of sensitivity that I had never experienced before.

As I reminisced about this pivotal moment, I decided to see if I could bring the same sensitivity and alertness that I had in the golf swing to the simple act of eating breakfast. I started with just holding the fork. I held the fork very lightly so I could feel its weight. The more gently I held the fork, the more sensitive to its weight I became. Thought was not operating; only sensitivity to what I was doing at that moment was operating. I brought this sensitivity to every action involved in the meal. Chewing the food was a whole new experience. Every bite was an explosion of flavor. The more gently and sensitively I chewed, the more I was able to feel the food in my mouth and all its subtle textures. Usually, my meals were rushed and I ate so fast that I barely tasted the food. When thought was quiet, all my senses seemed to be heightened. I was hearing all the voices in the diner simultaneously and smelling everything at once. I was seeing the faces of the patrons in such detail that it felt like I was seeing people for the first time. My gaze was so sensitive that I could see every wrinkle on their faces and every hair on their heads. I was truly in a state of complete awareness and sensitivity. Everything was bright and alive, unlike anything I had ever seen before. I left the diner in a true state of wonder. Every step I took down the street was with care and sensitivity. I felt as though each step was a precious gift to enjoy and feel. After a few hours of being in this state of awareness, the realities of life began to creep back in as my mind once again was filled with thought. I looked at the time—I was late for work!

The whole time at work I couldn't stop thinking about what had just happened to me. Was I losing my mind? It sure seemed like I was. The mind I had known for all my years was now operating in a totally different way. At that moment, I made another discovery. This alertness or awareness I had discovered was a mirror into who I truly was. My life was not alert or sensitive or gentle; my life was everything opposite of that. My life was a constant struggle and lacked any real depth. I had no time for sensitivity or gentleness. But in this other state, I was alive and alert. I was having a complete transformation of myself without even trying to do it! Once I was alert and sensitive, I had no problem staying in that state. It felt very natural, in contrast to what I could now see was my normal life. In my normal activities, I was never aware or sensitive. I was aggressive and in a constant state of effort—effort to achieve, effort to control, effort to make life the way I wanted it. The ability to see this duality was incredible and frustrating. I could see why people all over the world were constantly fighting and arguing. People had become attached to ideas and beliefs, just as I had in golf, only they were doing it in religion, politics and anything else they could form beliefs about. These attachments to ideas and beliefs were the very thing that masked sensitivity and awareness. The human race appeared to be an entire species with no real understand-

ing of sensitivity and, as a result, no ability to truly experience love in every action.

The more I became sensitive with all my actions, the more sensitive my interactions became with other people. I kept sharing this discovery with everyone I came in contact with. I started speaking with sensitivity, which was very strange because my whole vocabulary changed. Now, every word that left my mouth was said with care and awareness. People would listen to what I was saying with amazement. They wanted to know: Where did I learn this? … Who taught me this? The truth was no one taught me. I discovered it on my own in a moment of insight. The more sensitive I became, the clearer things became. I had a total metamorphosis of the mind, and it took no effort. It was a true joy becoming this new person, whereas in the past, trying to break a bad habit or trying to be a better person was a terrible struggle and tremendous effort.

During these days of discovery, I stayed in contact with Ralph, sharing everything with him. He, too, was having the same experience. We talked about life in a way that I had never discussed with anyone before. For the first time ever, my life felt like it had depth. Little did I know it was about to get much deeper.

CHAPTER
11

Art is not a thing it is a way
– Elbert Hubbard

THE DAYS HAD COME and gone and it was time for my U.S. Open qualifying tournament. I had not touched a club in over two weeks, but I felt as though I had been practicing all along—only this time, the practice was with my mind. I enlisted my new co-worker, Dan Gomery, to be my caddie. Dan was also a golfer who had been practicing various golf techniques for the past few years, but with little success. He thought technique was the answer because he was a master at Wing Chun martial arts, and this was the way martial arts had been taught for thousands of years. Dan wanted to come see what would happen when technique was abandoned and freedom was released.

As I stood on the first tee of the Illini Country Club, I felt something very unusual: a sense of peace. I usually felt very nervous and anxious, always thinking about my technique and whether it would hold up, and making sure I remembered to focus on what I had been working on. This time I was as calm as I could be. I looked at the fairway, planted my tee and ball, and without hesitation, took a swing. The ball sailed beautifully straight into the right rough, about 280 yards out.

I was on my way and the fact that the ball landed in the rough didn't faze or disappoint me in the least. In fact, I felt great about the shot. I took a bogey on that hole, as well as the next three holes. Not once was I upset or angry. I had a total sense of peace with the whole process. Before, I would have been very frustrated with bogeys and would have pressed to make birdies so I could catch up to the leaders, something that usually compounded the problems. On the fifth hole, I made my first par, which felt no better than the bogeys before it. Then on the tenth hole, as I was standing over a 35-foot putt for my first birdie of the day, I felt my mind fall into that deeply alert state. I could hear and feel everything. I gazed at the ball and the hole and without any conscious effort, I hit the ball. The ball rolled in what seemed like slow motion toward the hole. It appeared as if the hole was a magnet and the ball was being drawn toward it. Unable to escape its pull, the ball fell right into the hole. A cheer came from the small crowd surrounding us.

My playing partner that day was Illinois' No. 1 junior amateur, so a large group of spectators had come to watch him, including the head golf coach of one of the top universities in the state. Over the next five holes, I was a birdie machine. I chipped in for birdie, sank a few short putts and got myself back to even par.

As we headed to the seventeenth tee, the golf coach approached me and said, "Hell of a round you have going! Would you mind if I have a talk with you after the round is over?" I was a bit surprised at this but accepted his invite nonetheless. Why would such an esteemed golf coach want to speak with me? I quickly dismissed the thought and went back to my game. Under normal conditions, I would have been furious that someone had interrupted me during such an important round, but today I was fine with it. Because I just birdied the previous hole, I had the honor on the tee. It was a short hole, maybe 340 yards, but had trouble everywhere.

The long hitters could try for the green, but I reached for my 5 wood and proceeded to make an effortless swing, which sent the ball dead center 240 yards out. The other two players hit the ball right, landing in some very tall grass, a real predicament to say the least!

As my caddie, Dan, and I waited for the other two players to hit, I began to feel a connection to the next shot. I told Dan that I was going to put this ball in the hole from right there. Dan smirked and said, "Sure, OK." My bold prediction wasn't my ego talking. The same magnetism I felt on the first birdie of the day was once again present. I took my sand wedge from 100 yards and swung. The ball never left the flagstick. It landed maybe a foot from the hole and disappeared! The crowd erupted with applause. I looked at Dan, and with the biggest smile on his face, he dropped to his knees and began bowing and saying, "I'm not worthy!" It was truly a hilarious, yet defining, moment. When we reached the hole, I was surprised to see the ball out of the cup and on the back side. The ball had hit the stick but somehow went around the back of the cup and was hidden from our view by the flagstick, giving the appearance it had gone in. It hadn't! I was one inch away. As I walked to the eighteenth tee, my mind did something it hadn't done all day—it began to think. I was thinking "... if that ball had gone in for eagle and I had birdied the eighteenth ... I might have had a real shot at making it to the next stage of the U.S. Open qualifying." My mind was consumed with these thoughts. I addressed the ball and hit it straight left into the woods, leaving me with a double bogey to finish my round. Surprisingly, I wasn't disappointed. I was learning and realizing just how powerful thought was, seeing firsthand the power of thought and what it could do to a golf game. Honestly, I was more interested in talking to the golf coach who had approached me two holes earlier.

Dan and I met up with the coach in the parking lot. He immediately said he had never seen anyone play like that be-

fore. He kept saying how effortless it looked. I tried explaining to him what I had learned and how I discovered this understanding. When I finished speaking, he looked at me with utter confusion. I could see that what I was saying was not something his mind could comprehend. The coach congratulated me once again, said it was an honor to have witnessed such a remarkable round of golf, and wished me luck in the future. That was that. We shook hands and parted ways.

As I got in the car to head back to the city, it hit me that Ralph was probably finishing up his round about now. I was sure Ralph had qualified. How could he not? He did, after all, have two full weeks to practice. I tried calling Ralph several times on the ride home, but my calls kept going to voicemail. This meant one of two things: either he had not finished yet or he didn't make the cut and didn't want to talk to anyone. You see, golf at any level becomes a game of emotions. Putting all your energies into practice and then falling short can make a person ill with disgust and anger. It can truly make you feel like an utter failure. I knew this could not be the case with Ralph, though, because he was playing far too good leading up to this event. Then all of a sudden the phone rang. It was Ralph. "I made it! I shot 67 and came in second!!" I felt such tremendous joy in my heart for my friend's accomplishment as well as my own. We spoke for a few more minutes, then Ralph asked me if I would join him in Memphis in two weeks as his caddie for the final stage of qualifying. I felt like we were together on this journey, and I wasn't going to miss it for the world.

The next two weeks leading up to the second stage of qualifying were interesting to say the least. I began bringing more attention to each and every one of my actions. At work, I was moving the scenery and props with care and sensitivity. I was experiencing things at a deeper level. Everything had life, not just the living things. It was truly amazing. I began questioning everything and everyone. Backstage at work during downtime, a small group of stagehands and actors would sit in a small circle and discuss life. I would generally start the conversations asking very deep penetrating questions about life. What do you think love is? Why are humans violent? I kept trying to see if people could challenge themselves to ask difficult questions about life and its very meaning. Was their conditioning so hardwired that they could not put down their beliefs for even a moment to challenge themselves? I had been taught all my life what to think. Now I was beginning to question all of it. Maybe the real problem was that we are never taught how to think. This critical questioning was now easy for me but seemed terribly hard for most of the people I came into contact with. The fact that most people could not grasp what I was saying did not deter me in the least. In fact, it intrigued me. Instead of getting angry or frustrated, I began to feel a real sense of love for them. I would very calmly listen to their arguments against what I was saying and then respond with gentleness and care. No matter how upset someone got, I remained peaceful and calm. This approach evoked a more open, pliable conversation. I was able to see that trying to defend my position was what caused all conflict in the first place. I was not defending anything. On the contrary, I was just pointing out facts and forcing people to look at them. It was an eye-opening experience and had a resounding effect on the people around me.

During my free time in the evenings after work, I began experimenting with art. I realized that art was like the golf swing, with an idea or belief guiding the artist. So instead of sitting down to draw a certain picture based on my own thought, I would sit down to a blank sheet of paper and just draw whatever came out. With a rainbow of pastels, I just let my mind express itself without any direction. If I picked up the color pink and started drawing circles, so be it. I was accepting whatever came out. I just let freedom express itself. The results were amazing. I began drawing really strange

shapes and designs. Then within a few days, I was drawing human figures. Because I was not controlling the action, I had to wait awhile to see what picture was taking form. Then out of nowhere, I would see it … a dancing woman wearing a long gown. How could I, a man barely able to draw stick figures, create such beautiful art? These pictures, emanating from a totally free action, were being produced at a very fast rate as well. I could draw a picture in less than an hour and most times even quicker.

I began showing my art to the small group at work. They were skeptical when I told them I had no artistic training and that I drew these in a matter of hours. I could sense their hesitation, so I decided to show them right then and there. I found some acrylic paints and told the group I would paint a picture on the front of my tool box. I had never used actual paint before, so I was curious to see what I could produce. I started on the left side of a 4-by-2-foot wooden tool box. Initially, nothing was taking shape other than a mishmash of colors. Finally, after about ten minutes of nothing and aware of everyone starring, I stopped. I asked myself if I was looking for a result or was I truly just creating? I saw instantly that I was trying to prove something to these people, so I let it go. I gently took my brush and began painting very carefully on the empty right side panel. Within thirty minutes I had drawn Jesus hanging on a cross. The image was a little disturbing, to say the least, as it included blood from his wounds and his emaciated body. Everyone kept asking why I chose to paint that particular picture. I assured them I was not a practitioner of any specific religion; in fact, I was telling everyone about the dangers of religion—how people had misused religion to divide us and how it contributes to disorder in the world.

I learned all this by continuing to ask myself: What would happen if I let go of beliefs or ideas? Time and time again I

**You can view Noah's art at Peaceful-golf on Facebook*

saw the cause of conflict was my attachment to an idea or belief. If letting go of this gave me freedom, why would I want any ideas or beliefs? We are conditioned to believe that freedom means making our own choices in life. I was starting to see that real freedom was not making a choice at all. The moment I made a choice, I was moving in a very specific path toward that choice, narrowing my freedom and movement. Instead of being able to move in all directions at once, I was only able to move in whatever direction my choice would allow. If I gave up choice, all avenues became open to exploration. This was truly a liberating feeling, and I was seeing what real freedom meant.

CHAPTER 12

There can be no deep disappointment where there is not deep love
– Martin Luther King, Jr.

TWO WEEKS HAD PASSED and it was now time to make my way to Memphis and join Ralph for the final stage of the U.S. Open qualifying at the Colonial Country Club. Colonial is a thirty-six hole facility and one of the finest in the area. Both courses offer uniquely different golf challenges. The North Course is a par-71 measuring 6,646 yards from the back tees. A variety of golf shots are required from tee to green on the North Course. With tree-lined zoysia fairways and Emerald Bermuda greens, the North Course is a pleasure to play but remains challenging for golfers of every skill level. The South Course, a par-72 measuring 7,334 from the back tees, is without question one of the most challenging courses in the country and one of the most enjoyable. With tree-lined fairways, Champion Bermuda greens, gorgeous lakes, and elevation changes uncharacteristic to the region, the South Course is truly a gem.

The qualifying was being held on both courses with competitors playing each 18 holes once for a total of 36 holes in one day. We had drawn the South Course to start, which meant if

Ralph played a good round there, the U.S. Open berth might just be attainable. Upon arriving at the parking lot, I was met by my very alert friend, eager to get started. Ralph had been trying to get to this level for quite some time, and now the opportunity was here. As I approached him, Ralph asked me if I could feel "it." To which I replied, "yes." The feeling was that of two people in effortlessness, in tune with themselves and each other. Our bodies and minds were about to experience a round of golf not many will ever relate to.

Ralph and I headed into the pro shop to sign in and ask about the course conditions. The pro informed us that the course was playing firm and fast and that our group was teeing off right on time. As we left the pro shop and headed for the driving range, we walked past none other than Steve Elkington, PGA Tour winner! Then we saw Brandt Snedeker! I was surrounded by some of the best golfers in world. Memphis is a unique qualifying location for the U.S. Open. That same week in Memphis, the PGA Tour was running its St. Jude Classic. Anyone outside the top 50 in the world must qualify for the U.S. Open. Since all the tour pros were in town for the St. Jude Classic, most of the qualifiers that day were PGA Tour players. As a result, the USGA gave twenty qualifying spots, rather than the normal four. The top twenty lowest scores would be advancing to the U.S. Open. Top 20 seemed very doable in my eyes. As we headed to the horseshoe-style driving range, Ralph and I both remained silent. The range was filled with some of the best professional golfers in the world—players who had won numerous tour events and some who had even reached top 20 in the world. There were no open stalls except right in the middle. I was standing in complete awe among all these world-class golfers.

Ralph pulled a wedge out of the bag and started to hit balls at a flagstick about 75 yards away. On his second shot he rattled the flagstick, not an uncommon sound on a range with so many pros. But then he did it again and again! At

that point I looked around and noticed everyone starring at Ralph. Feeling a bit uneasy with the attention, Ralph said to me, "Let's get out of here."

We headed to the putting green right near the first tee. While Ralph worked on his putting, I went through his bag to make sure we had the correct number of clubs and everything necessary for this five-hour walk. As I looked around at the grounds, I felt the same sense of awareness and energy that I felt a few weeks ago while playing golf with Johnny. I was once again in a true state of effortlessness. I could see that Ralph was feeling the same way. The proof was in his actions; he was calm, alert and totally present. He touched the earth and his clubs with a sense of respect and understanding. The time finally came for us to tee off. The round that would change our lives was about to begin. We said little as Ralph approached the first tee. It was early in the morning, dew was still on the ground, and you could see the mist rising as it evaporated. The air was clean and filled with the scent of freshly cut grass.

The first and tenth tees were adjacent to each other, so we needed to make sure no one was teeing off on No. 10, so as not to make any noise while they were hitting. The group on 10 had just teed off, and we were all set to let it rip. Ralph took out his driver and proceeded to hit the most beautiful drive straight down the middle of this long par-5. As we walked down the downward-sloping fairway, we saw a ball sitting right in the middle. As we approached, I had the feeling that this could not be Ralph's ball because he hit it way too good. He checked the ball and his marking—a Titleist with a red "4" and a green dot that he had added for identification. Much to my surprise, Ralph said, "Yep, this is my ball." Then he proceeded to hit away. Not a minute went by when we were met on the course by PGA Tour pro Jimmy Smart, who was coming from the woods to the left, looking for his ball. He had just teed off on No. 10 and sliced his drive into Ralph's fairway. We discovered another ball about 30 yards in front of where Ralph had just hit. We assumed this one was Jimmy's ball and wished him luck on the rest of his round. Ralph and I then walked ahead and finished the first hole.

After two pars on the first couple holes, Ralph approached the third hole, which was a long par 4. Just then, a rules official pulled up in a golf cart. She walked to the tee and right up to us. Pulling out a Titleist golf ball—with a red "4" and green dot on the top, identical to the one Ralph was playing—she pointedly asked Ralph, "Is this yours?" Reaching into his pocket and pulling out what he thought was his ball, Ralph said, "No, that's not mine. This is mine." The ball he was holding had the same markings as the ball the official had. I stood there watching this thinking, what are the odds?!

The official explained that Jimmy Smart said he sliced his tee shot on 10 into Ralph's fairway and that Ralph mistakenly hit his ball and vice versa. Ralph protested, saying that was not possible and that he had been using the same ball from the start of the tournament. It's one player's word over another. The official abruptly returned to her cart and drove away with the problem unresolved. Ralph was understandably upset and confused, as was I. How was this possible? How can two players have the same ball with the same markings in the same place and just happen to be in such close proximity to each other that they mistakenly hit each other's ball?

Ralph teed it up and hit a great shot down the middle, but his mind was now elsewhere. If the ball that the official was holding turned out to be his, Ralph's round—and chance to qualify for the U.S. Open—would be over. If, indeed, he finished the first hole with the wrong ball and did not correct his error before teeing off the second hole, he would be disqualified immediately. Had he gone back and played another ball from the correct spot (before teeing off on the second hole), he would have been penalized just two shots.

As we walked to his tee shot on the third hole, Ralph looked at me with a worried expression and said, "Noah, I think that might have been my ball that the official showed us." It was hard for us to accept, but the possibility was definitely there, especially since we both thought it odd how short Ralph was on the first drive of the day. Right at that moment, I felt a true sense of peace over myself and told Ralph that this was out of our hands and all we could do was finish this round and wait for the rules team to decide our fate. We got this far; we should finish and see what the golf gods had in store for us. Let's just finish this round with love and sensitivity. Ralph agreed. He immediately fell into that state of creative love and started hitting incredible golf shots. He was sticking it close and knocking it in. By the time we reached the fourteenth hole, we were 5-under and in the proverbial zone. The fourteenth was a shorter par 4 with an uphill approach on the second shot into the green. Ralph hit a great tee ball that landed on the left side of the fairway, about 160 yards from the hole. When I handed Ralph his 9 iron, I felt something special was about to happen. It reminded me of when I hit that wedge a few weeks earlier in my qualifier, the shot that almost resulted in an eagle. Ralph took his swing and while the ball was in midair, he said aloud, "Oh man, please be good!" With a sense of calm assurance I said, "It is." A second later, the ball hit the bottom of the cup and totally blew the whole side of the cup out. The hole was destroyed so badly that the grounds crew had to come and move it! This round was becoming the stuff of legends.

By the time we got to the eighteenth hole, a massive crowd had gathered around the green, and Ralph had one last birdie attempt to try to shoot a 63. It was a 20-footer that had a few curls and twists. That same sense of peace and calm I had felt earlier in the day was still with me. It was right then that Ralph struck the ball, and I watched it slide just by the edge of the cup. Ralph tapped the putt in and carded a 64.

We had both totally forgotten about the whole ball situation ... well, at least until we started walking to the scoring tent. It was there that we were once again met by the same rules official who spoke with us earlier.

She said to Ralph, without the least bit of compassion, "You are disqualified." What? Ralph just shot a 64! How could he be disqualified? There must be some mistake. "I'm sorry, but another official said he saw you hit the wrong ball and that's the end of it." Ralph broke down in tears. There would be no second round on the shorter, easier course; there would be no U.S. Open in his future. He could not believe what had just happened. His parents and friends had all come to cheer him on, but it was no help. Ralph was inconsolable. I, too, was in a state of shock. How was this possible? If there was another spotter who saw this, then why did they not come out and tell us on that hole? Why were we not told until the third hole? All of this was so strange and truly upsetting.

It was at that moment, while I was standing by myself just pondering the situation and the day as a whole, that Ralph's father approached me. "Noah, I just want to thank you. In the past few weeks since you showed Ralph whatever it is you found—your effortless approach—he has become another person. He has never been so happy and centered. He seems humble yet confident. It is truly remarkable; I don't quite understand it, but keep it up." I shook his hand and we spoke for a moment about how much this disqualification hurt all of us. A few minutes later, we were all in the parking lot saying our goodbyes. Ralph was feeling better, and we both knew this was only the beginning of the journey. This experience would not defeat either of us. To this day, that was the best round of tournament golf I have ever seen. I left with the feeling that great things were in store for us, both in golf and in life.

CHAPTER 13

It is hard to fail, but it is worse never to have tried to succeed
– Theodore Roosevelt

RALPH CALLED ME the following week to tell me that he was going to sign up for PGA Tour Q-School. He felt his game was good, and seeing how well he played under pressure, I knew he couldn't be stopped. This was great news to hear. I told Ralph that if he needed a caddie, I would be more than happy to oblige. I was still on the road with my Broadway touring job but would be in San Francisco on the same dates as Q-School. If Ralph chose San Fran for his qualifying, I would just take those days off from work to be his caddie. Ralph thought this was a great idea. It was still four months away, so he had plenty of time to practice and hone this new-found understanding. I, on the other hand, was exploring all the ways this could work in other aspects of life, not just golf. When Ralph finally arrived in San Fransisco we had been working on effortlessness, as I called it, for around six months. For most of that time, I concentrated on my artwork and talking to others about my discovery. I had so much passion about what I was learning and experiencing that I couldn't help but share. Golf took a momentary backseat, and I simply played for fun.

Ralph had been taking the same approach back in Arkansas. But now he was in California to try to qualify for the PGA Tour. I had agreed to drive down and stay with him near the course. We would get to play a couple practice rounds and hopefully scout enough of the course to give ourselves a real chance. I was very hopeful that Ralph would have a great showing, seeing how well he did only a few months earlier at the U.S. Open tryouts. This was a whole different game though. This was 150 guys who had each paid $5,000 for the chance to get on the PGA Tour. Only thirty of those players would be moving on to the next stage. The PGA Q-School consisted of three stages, each one taking only the top players from the previous stage.

We were playing a course called San Juan Oaks Golf Club, a Fred Couples design, in Hollister, California, about an hour from Pebble Beach. The course was one I had played before and recommended to Ralph. It was a solid length at 7,133 yards with all the danger right in front of you, so course knowledge wasn't going to be that big of a deal.

We played a couple practice rounds, but Ralph was struggling a bit. He told me he was feeling immense pressure. He said he was putting everything he had into this and didn't know what he was going to do if he lost this tournament. He was nearly out of money and time. Bills were piling up and life was passing him by, one lost tournament after another. I looked at him and saw someone whose mind was cluttered, racing, unsure. This had me really concerned because I knew all too well that the only way effortlessness could work was with a mind free of thought—a mind clear and quiet.

Ralph had neither. And because of this, his fate in the tournament was sealed before he took his first swing. When I first revealed the effortless approach to Ralph months ago, I told him to stop trying all the swing techniques he had learned his whole life, to stop cluttering his mind with previous instruction and thoughts on how to swing and how not to

swing. But looking at him that day, all I could see was someone in a desperate state. He was heading into his most important tournament with the baggage of having to perform well. This, to me, was a recipe for disaster. Sure enough, Ralph shot well over par on the first two days, essentially ending any hope of moving on.

This failure was hard for him to accept, but I was able to realize that looking for a result was the real culprit that led to his high scores and downfall. I tried sharing all this with Ralph, but he was in no frame of mind to absorb what I was saying. Over the next eight months, I didn't hear from Ralph that much. He put his sticks down and took some time off from golf.

CHAPTER 14

Love is all we have, the only way that each can help the other
– Euripides

A FEW MONTHS after the tournament, I began to question if what I was doing in life was right. I was starting to realize that people were not just listening to what I was saying; they were starting to look to me for answers. This was a real problem for me, because I realized early on that following people was what had gotten me into trouble in the first place. By following other ideas and opinions about golf, I was sacrificing my own psychological freedom. Freedom of the mind was my main concern and the thing I enjoyed sharing with others the most. People didn't want to discover freedom on their own, it seemed. They wanted me to show them how to do it; much in the same way I wanted a teacher to show me how to hit the ball correctly.

I started to become very confused about what direction to move in. I wanted to share with people, but I certainly didn't want to be anyone's authority. I could see I truly didn't have total freedom and I was still learning every day. I had my own ups and downs just like anyone else. At the same time all this was happening, my job was coming to an end, because the

tour was wrapping up. I decided that before I took another step forward, I should have a clear plan about how to proceed. Should I give lectures on effortlessness? Should I play golf? Should I go back and do Broadway shows? I was in a state of confusion. Freedom had shaken my whole foundation, and it was only the beginning.

I decided to move back to Arkansas so I could share my discovery with David Lee and work on my game, all the while still trying to figure things out. David listened to all I had to say but felt I still needed the technical aspect as well as the mental aspect to play the game at a high level. Cricket was much more receptive to my approach and allowed herself to question her own beliefs about life and religion. This time in Arkansas was a totally different experience. I was no longer hitting thousands of balls a day. Instead, I was only practicing occasionally with most of my time spent challenging those around me. I would ask everyone I came in contact with what they thought real freedom was. Most of the time I was met with the same response of "freedom is the ability to choose what you want to do at any time." I was saying just the opposite: Anytime you made a choice, you were actually giving up your freedom. Choice to me was a limitation and a sign of confusion.

I knew that what I was saying was contrary to everything they had been taught growing up. I knew the only way I could break down these conditioned responses was to approach everything with love. This was never more evident than the morning I stayed home and slept in. I woke up around 9 a.m. and looked out my front window to check the weather when I saw an older gentleman at the end of my driveway out for a walk. He had a cane and was seemingly conversing with my neighbor from a distance. I was curious, so I went out to get my mail and further observe. We exchanged hellos and I told him I had just moved into the neighborhood and would be staying for a few months. He told me he was a deacon at a church in Little Rock. This to me was a perfect chance to talk to a man of the cloth about the lack of freedom I felt religion offered and see what he thought. I asked him if he minded if I walked with him for a bit and if we could talk. He smiled and motioned me to walk with him.

I began sharing with him how we never touch life with gentleness and care in all our actions. How we are never truly free if we follow a religion or a belief. I was in a true effortless state while talking to him. He let me talk the whole time, never interrupting me. When I was done, he wanted to know who taught me this. I told him this was the first thing in life I had discovered on my own. He immediately said I needed to come to his home and meet his wife. She was a missionary and would certainly want to hear what I had to say.

When we arrived at their home, I was greeted by a very nice woman who invited me in with open arms. Her husband explained to her how I had approached him and that I had something to share. She sat down and listened to me talk about love and freedom for at least thirty minutes. The whole time, the deacon was smiling from ear to ear. When I finished, she stared at me and said, "I have only one question for you. Do you accept Jesus Christ as your savior?" I was shocked. I had just shared how any religion or belief was a roadblock to real freedom and love, and here she was asking about Jesus as my savior.

Being in a state of freedom allowed me to answer the question with nothing but love. I told her that I entered her home without any beliefs or ideas, only a state of love. If I said that I do accept Jesus then that belief would separate me from all those who don't. If I reject Christ, then I would push away all those who do believe in him. I told her I saw that belief was the very thing keeping us from loving each other and that I was now able to see the true danger of all beliefs; therefore, I could not answer that question.

"I can only say I came into your home with love in my

heart and I will leave the same way." She shook her head and left the room. I began to walk to the door to leave when the deacon approached me. "Noah, I have been in the church my whole life, and you have upended everything I held true with your talk. Don't stop sharing with people. What you have to say is far too important for this world." We shared a big hug, and off I went with a heart full of love. Yes, I was disappointed that his wife was unable to hear what I was saying, but I knew that her husband did hear it, and that was enough for me to know I was exactly where I needed to be in my life.

I ended up spending seven months in Arkansas and thought I was starting to understand what to do with my life. I decided I would move to Phoenix, Arizona, to teach golf and share this message of freedom and love. I chose Phoenix because it was one of the best golf destination cities I had visited during all my years of touring. I also thought it would give me a great chance at finding a large group of students to teach. I figured people would want to learn Effortless Golf, and at the same time, I would be offering my knowledge about life and the possibilities of real freedom.

CHAPTER 15

How ridiculous and how strange to be surprised at anything which happens in life
– Marcus Aurelius

BEFORE I LEFT for Phoenix, I received an unexpected call from Ralph saying he signed up to play in the Monday qualifier for the PGA Tour's St. Jude Classic. He asked me to come caddie for him, and I gladly said yes. His call came a little out of left field since I knew Ralph hadn't touched a club in months. This tournament was an interesting choice because it was exactly one year to the day from the U.S. Open disaster. In fact, the tour qualifier would be held on the same day as the U.S. Open qualifier and in the same town of Memphis, Tennessee.

I think Ralph was too heartbroken to try for the Open again, so this was a good way to get back into the game he loved. I made the trip to Memphis without any expectations for Ralph, and when I saw him at the course, I knew he had none either. He was relaxed, in a good mood, and said he was there to enjoy himself. From the first swing of the day, Ralph was hitting it pure. Shot after shot and putt after putt, he kept pouring it into the hole. When we reached the seventeenth hole, a tough par-3, we were 6-under and in the top five or

six players. The only problem was you needed to finish in the top four to qualify for the PGA tournament that week.

Up until then, Ralph and I really hadn't said much to each other. We were just enjoying the day. Ralph took forever choosing a club and then hit one of the worst shots of the day, straight in the water to the right of the green. He took a drop and salvaged a bogey, but the damage was done. On the eighteenth tee, Ralph turned to me and said, "We need a birdie to get in I think." OK, then do it! Ralph proceeded to hit his worst drive of the day, straight up the right side and under a tree. In fact, this shot was lying on the root of the tree! We assessed the shot and Ralph took a full rip at it. The ball came out super low and tracked right at the pin, rolling onto the green. What a shot! When we got to the green I could see Ralph was really nervous, evident by his shaking hands. He wanted this birdie so bad, but he choked and blew it 5 feet by the hole. With the pressure on, he managed to make a comeback putt to finish with a 67. We both assumed he had probably missed his chance, so when we went into the scoring booth, we were shocked to see he was officially in fourth place, and no one was left on the course with a real chance. Ralph had just qualified for his first PGA Tour event, and I was part of it! We were both ecstatic.

After this great news, the change in Ralph's behavior was dramatic and instantaneous. He went from being in a state of effortlessness to someone who was now edgy and scattered. His cool, calm demeanor had quickly vanished. His focus shifted to a long "to do" list: registering with the PGA Tour right away, booking a hotel room, calling his family and friends, and most importantly, scheduling a practice round for the next day. Ralph was overwhelmed and it showed. I had just witnessed the craziness that the tour and the prospect of winning big money could do to someone.

That night we checked in at the PGA Tour room at the TPC Southwind in Memphis. Everyone was very welcoming and they gave us a complementary vehicle to use for the week.

We enjoyed a nice but hasty dinner since Ralph still had a few things to do, and we were scheduled to tee off at 7 a.m. the next day.

CHAPTER 16

The proud person always wants to do the right thing, the great thing. But because he wants to do it in his own strength, he is fighting not with man, but with God
– Søren Kierkegaard

THE NEXT DAY CAME, and what a day it was! Tuesdays were for practice rounds, and being the new guys, we were one of the first groups to head out on the course. But first, though, Ralph decided to warm up a little. First stop, the putting green. Ralph dropped three balls on the green and tried to putt a 10-footer. All three balls rolled about 20 feet away from the cup and nearly off the green! These were the fastest greens we had ever seen. If Ralph had one weakness in his game it was putting; he was streaky. I could see this rattled his nerves. It took about ten minutes for Ralph to acclimate to the greens, but once that happened, he quickly got the speed down. Even so, this was going to be a whole new game with greens this fast.

Shortly after, we moved over to the range and started to warm up the full swing. Ralph registered his name and was then asked what type of ball he wanted to hit. The array of practice golf balls was mind-boggling; any brand of ball you wanted to hit, they had. Even cooler was when they put Ralph's name on a plaque adjacent to Vijay Singh. I was giving swing advice to my friend Ralph, who was hitting practice balls right next to a two-time major winner. All I can say is, Vijay was even smoother in person than he appears on TV.

Ralph was hitting it great, just smoothing it out there with no effort at all. Finally, with nobody to join us, we headed to the first tee for our very quiet practice round. The practice round was uneventful, just two friends walking a course, trying all kinds of different shots. We were simply enjoying ourselves and observing the course. The course at Southwind is notorious for being difficult. In fact, it generally plays as one of the hardest tour stops all year. Average winning scores are minus-4 to 4-over. This tournament takes place two weeks before the U.S. Open, so the PGA Tour purposely made the course more challenging than most to prepare players for what was to come. The rough was thick and the greens were lightning fast.

After the practice round was over, we went back to the range and were met by some of the club manufacturers, who were more than happy to outfit Ralph with tons of new equipment, all for free. He got a brand new set of clubs, a new bag, some clothes, etc. A lot of these companies were giving everything and anything to Ralph on the off chance that he would win the tournament or finish high enough so the world would see him playing and wearing their gear.

While we were trying out one of the new drivers, a member from the PGA Tour approached Ralph about playing in the pro-am on Wednesday. They would pay him $2,500 to participate. The money would be a huge help for a guy who hadn't cashed a check in over a year. The only problem was playing in the pro-am would mean a day away from the course and missing a practice round. The pro-am would be held at a country club down the street from Southwind. Given his financial situation, Ralph decided to take the cash and play the pro-am. I understood his decision but was not thrilled about it. Missing that practice round would prove to be a mistake.

Sure enough, when he came back the next day from the pro-am, Ralph was dejected and in a mental funk because he shot a 76 and said he played terrible. Playing in a pro-am before his first PGA Tour event was certainly the wrong approach, but I was in no position to be telling Ralph what to do. I had never been in a PGA Tour event either, and this was a learning experience for us both.

The next day came early, as we were one of the first groups to start the tournament. We started on the tenth tee with almost no one in the stands. Ralph hit his first drive straight down the middle and saved a nice par from a greenside bunker. Considering how difficult this hole was, walking away with par seemed like a birdie. The round was going pretty well for the first eight holes. As we arrived on the eighteenth, our ninth hole, Ralph pulled a driver for this sharp dogleg left around a lake. Without an ounce of fear, he hit the ball straight over the water, landing it right in the center of the fairway, about 140 yards out. The other two players in our group pulled 5 woods on this very long par-4 hole and bailed out to the right, avoiding the challenging water altogether, leaving themselves about 200 yards in. When I look back on it now, I realize that particular shot Ralph hit was one of the hardest shots on the course, and the veterans, unlike us, recognized it immediately. Sometimes ignorance truly is bliss.

When we got to the ball, we started assessing the shot selections. We finally agreed a good 9 iron would do the trick. As I backed away with the bag, I bumped into this guy with a giant microphone. He was listening to our whole conversation—we were on live TV! Both Ralph and I smiled at each other. He approached the shot with about 200 onlookers and God knows how many TV viewers. Because it was the eighteenth green, there were grandstands surrounding it. Ralph struck the ball perfectly, and in an instant, it was flying at the pin. Then all we heard was crack! The ball had hit the stick and ricocheted off about eight feet away. The crowd went wild, and we high-fived each other. Maybe this tournament was ours to win. Up in the TV booth, Ralph's shot caught the attention of the well-known golf-pro-turned-announcer Sir Nick Faldo, who exclaimed "Great shot from a Monday qualifier named Ralph Raines! Now let's see if he can make that putt. That's where this game is won and lost."

The pressure was on. Unfortunately, Ralph proceeded to miss the putt. He started the back nine at 2-over but was by no means out of this thing. The back nine was a different story, though. Ralph really struggled coming into the final holes and carded a 6-over 78. I thought he really played great considering all the nerves and it being his first time. He, however, was not happy, and I felt the same negative emotions I witnessed from him seven months earlier at Q-School.

As we were leaving the course, Ralph decided he wanted to practice putting for a while, so we hit the putting green. There were tons of pros practicing and we found one hole to ourselves. We talked about the round and shared some stories about the day. As we were talking, we saw Vijay hitting chip shots just off the green about twenty feet from us. He proceeded to hit full-swing flop shots that were going about fifteen feet in the air but only traveling about five feet forward! Now this isn't the hardest shot in the world for a pro, but to do it while all your peers are standing on the green and knowing if you catch it just a hair thin you could possibly kill someone… well, that was quite a feat! I stood in awe and said to myself, we are not worthy, just as Dan had done with me the year before, caddying at my U.S. Open qualifier.

The next day we had a late tee time, so we met at the course around 10 a.m. to get in some good practice. This day would be special because all of Ralph's friends and family would be there to support him. While I was on the range waiting for Ralph, I ran into Troy Matteson. I hadn't seen him since I was at Gravity Golf with David, a couple years earlier. Troy was a PGA Tour winner and was the leading

money winner on the Nationwide Tour one year. Troy visited Gravity Golf once to take a lesson from David, and we hit it off right away. He told me that my swing was plenty good to play on tour and that I should get out there and try more tournaments. I wasn't convinced at the time, as my scores were still not low enough, so I never took his advice to heart.

"Hey Noah, good to see you! What are you doing here?" asked Troy. I explained to him about my new teaching style, how Ralph was one of my students, and I was there coaching him, as well as caddying for him. Troy immediately said he'd love to hear more about my teaching and prompted me to give him a quick lesson. After a ten-minute lesson, it was apparent I needed more time with Troy for him to really grasp the whole approach I was offering. Most of the players on tour worked with a more technical, rather than a mental, approach, and it was the mental aspect that my teaching was centered around. Troy thanked me and wished me luck with my golf career. To this day, I still consider him to be a real class act and someone who could see my talent long before I could.

Soon after that, Ralph arrived at the range and we went to work. He was in better spirits after having a tough finish the day before. He was hitting the ball great and his putting was solid. When we arrived at the first tee, the stands where packed, certainly a new experience for us both. Ralph hit his tee shot into the right rough, and I would like to say it was the worst shot he hit all day, but unfortunately it was only one of many to come. Right from the start, he was scrambling, hitting shots unlike I had seen him hit before—slicing and hooking, missing putts by a mile, and just generally struggling. When we reached the fourteenth hole at plus-7, Ralph turned to me and said, "I'm done! I can't do this. I am embarrassing myself out here. I'm walking off the course."

I could feel his frustration and despair, but at the same time I could tell that, mentally, he was right back where he had been before, looking for another result instead of staying in the effortless moment. I told him that at this point, his score was irrelevant, since there was no way he could make the cut, let alone win the tournament. But there were still four holes to play, and to simply walk off the course at this point would not only be unprofessional, it would be selfish. I reminded Ralph that all of his friends and family who traveled long distances to see him play, did so not solely to see him win, but for the sheer pleasure and to support his dream of playing on the PGA Tour. He should be proud to have made it this far and to be playing with the best golfers in the world—not holding his head down, pouting and threatening to walk off the course. I looked at Ralph and very plainly said, "These people want to see your love and joy for the game." In an instant, he heard what I was saying, and I saw him slip into a state of effortlessness for the first time since the Monday qualifier.

He made some nice shots to finish off the round and even had a putt at eagle on sixteen that he ultimately missed but was nonetheless fun to witness. When the round was over, Ralph said that he didn't even want to know his score or hand it in. Instead, he hung around to sign a bunch of autographs for all the kids waiting by the practice tee. I was happy to see him embracing his last few moments on tour. Little did I know this would be the last competitive event Ralph would ever play in.

CHAPTER 17

The whole problem with the world is that fools and fanatics are always so certain of themselves, and wise people so full of doubts
– Bertrand Russell

RALPH QUIT competitive golf after that PGA Tour event. He became convinced that his failure was not mental but physical. He felt that because he was playing side by side with the best in the world, he could tell they were playing with a better technical move. He gave up not only on golf, but on effortlessness. I understood his disappointment, but I never understood, even to this day, his defeatist attitude. It's one thing to spend a few days after a tournament mulling over your bad performance. But to completely give up tournaments? This I did not understand and it drew me deeper into my discoveries and my own progression with the game of golf.

I decided to head back to New York for the summer and visit my family before heading to Phoenix. I would work hard on my golf game and try a Monday qualifier while I was home. I signed up for an upstate New York PGA Tour Monday qualifying event that was going to be held at the Indian casino, Turning Stone. The Monday qualifier would be held at one of the casino courses, while the actual tournament would be down the road at the sister course, Atunyote. The course I would be playing was called the Kaluhyat course, considered one of the toughest courses in the Northeast. It was 7,100 yards long with a slope rating of 151. The course wound its way through swampland and marsh, and from playing my practice round, I figured it was clear that a score of 2- or 3-under would more than likely be enough to advance.

I had never been someone who shot 63, but I was someone who could shoot a couple under on any type of track. So with a good location to play, I enlisted my friend Scott to come caddie for me. Scott had played many rounds with me in the past, and he himself was quite a good golfer when he was young. I picked Scott up early in the morning for our trip upstate. On the way, we had a nice talk about life and our friendship. We opened up to each other and had a real conversation. When we got to the course, I went straight to the range to warm up. On the first swing, I hit the ball perfectly, setting the standard for the rest of the day. Swing after swing, shot after shot ... perfection. While I was hitting, an older gentleman came up and introduced himself as Charlie Mitchell, one of the PGA Tour officials that day. "I just wanted to tell you that I have been watching you warm up, and you have the best swing of all the guys I've seen so far. I want to wish you luck, and I really hope you qualify." I was honored by his comments and thanked him. We chatted for a few more minutes, then I headed to the first tee. I couldn't help but smile—I was feeling confident with a real sense of freedom.

Scott was already at the first tee sizing up the field when he pointed out to me that, playing two groups in front of us, was none other than two-time U.S. Open winner Lee Janzen! Scott looked confused and said, "They make him Monday-qualify? I don't get it." I explained to Scott that tournament winners only have exemptions for a certain number of years (depending on the tournament) and then must return to Monday qualifying like the rest of the competitors. Scott still thought this was crazy, and to be honest, so did I. I

did think, however, it was pretty cool to be competing against a two-time U.S. Open champion!

On the first tee, I would be first to hit in our group. I felt myself fall into a state of effortlessness, and I approached the first shot with a sense of calm and gentleness that I had only felt a few times before while playing golf. I did not steer or guide the shot; I just swung effortlessly. I killed it dead center about 300 yards on the opening par-5. I turned to Scott and said, "Let's go see what happens." The second shot was a little over 250 yards and I took a 3 wood. I hit the ball just short of the green and watched it roll the rest of the way onto the green, leaving me with a 20-foot putt for eagle. I lipped out the eagle and started my round with a birdie!

I parred the next two holes and lipped out for birdie on the third. On the fourth hole, I came to the second par-5 of the day, a long dogleg right, with a drive over a lake. The water carry was long and had more trouble the closer you went toward the green. As I was waiting to tee off, one of the officials pulled up, and it turned out to be Charlie Mitchell. "Hey Noah! How's the round going?"

I smiled and said, "Pretty good, Charlie! I'm minus-1." Charlie stayed and watched me hit. I crushed it right down the most dangerous line. I carried the water and ended up dead center about 235 yards from the pin. Charlie drove behind us, watching all the action. My second shot was right at the stick, but unfortunately it was about 10 feet short, landing in the greenside bunker. I hit out of the bunker and nearly made the shot. The only thing now between me and a birdie was a 6-foot putt. Done—I hit it straight in. Charlie started clapping, then gave me a smile as he drove away.

After making another birdie on eight, I finished the front minus-3 on a brutally tough course. I managed a par on No. 10 by the skin of my teeth. On the eleventh hole, I hit it closest to the pin, only nine feet away. Both of my playing partners miraculously chipped it in from very precarious positions off the green. As I approached my putt, I said aloud, "Well now I have to make it!" I hit the ball perfectly and I watched it drop right in the hole. I was now 4-under. The twelfth hole was another par-5 that was considered the hardest on the course. The drive was from the top of a steep hill, across a stream to an island fairway. Then you still had over 300 yards left. I killed it dead center, then laid up to the 150-yard marker. The green, shaped like a volcano, was about thirty feet above the fairway. This was a tough shot with no room for error. I hit the shot flawlessly and just missed the flagstick on the fly. My ball ended up only five feet away. When the putt dropped, I was feeling ecstatic! I was 5-under par in a Monday qualifier, wanting to go lower.

As my group started walking to the next tee, one of my playing partners approached me and said, "Man you are one of the best players I've ever seen. Why aren't you on tour?" I told him a little of my story, but as I was speaking, my mind started to wander. Instead of being clear and effortless as it had been all day, my mind was now full of thought. He's right. Why am I not on tour? Probably because I never played this well under pressure. I'm not really that good, and my swing is bound to fail. With all these thoughts filling my once-quiet mind, I now tried to focus, but focus, as you will learn, cannot be forced.

On the next tee box, I looked to my left and said to myself, "Don't hit it over there, it's O.B." That was the first time all day I had allowed fear to enter my mind on the golf course. I swung and pulled the drive straight into the left trees out of bounds. I scrambled and made bogey and knew I was done. Scott saw that I was beginning to unravel and tried his best to encourage me, but it was no use. I had lost that precious state of effortlessness that had guided me throughout the day. Now it was gone, and I was back to playing my normal game.

I finished the round 3-over on the back nine for a round of 72 even par. As I walked off the eighteenth green toward

the clubhouse, I passed by the scoreboard. Lee Janzen was there waiting for the remaining groups to post their scores, as well as to see if his 3-under score was good enough to qualify. I was never so close to making my dream a reality and I allowed it to slip through my fingers. I was not broken by this event. In fact, I was even more inspired to understand why I fell apart and to find a way to improve my game. I decided now was the time to head to Phoenix to start teaching golf and see where effortlessness would lead.

CHAPTER 18

The mind is its own place, and in itself can make a Heaven of Hell, a Hell of Heaven
– John Milton

I ARRIVED IN PHOENIX with no set teaching job. I decided that I would start my search by paying a visit to the first driving range I found and hoped my resume and accolades would speak for themselves. Sure, I was nervous, but I had nothing to lose and needed to make this happen.

I found a public course only minutes from the apartment I was renting and went straight to the pro shop to speak with the head pro. His name was Doc Stickler, a rail-thin man around the age of 60. As I spoke to him about my background and my unique teaching method of Effortless Golf, I could see he wasn't being very responsive, and my odds of getting a job there were not looking too good. Then I mentioned that I was featured in Golf Digest and Golf Magazine, and the whole dynamic of the conversation changed. As soon as I showed Doc the magazines, he told me I could teach at either of the two courses he managed. I was so thrilled! I thanked him and was about to leave when he said to me, "Ya know, Noah, we have a weekly tournament going on right now, and a guy from my group just canceled. Why don't you join us?"

This was a local money game, and I was sure Doc was sizing me up, curious to see what I could deliver on the course—especially since I just talked myself up and showed him the magazines! Of course, I could not refuse the challenge. Luckily for me, I was on my game that day. I ended up shooting a 69 the first time I ever saw the course, and on the eighteenth hole, I made a great eagle, which I was confident would win me a skin. As we walked off the green, I turned to Doc and casually asked, "So do you think I'll win low score?"—all along thinking no one played better than I did that day.

"No, that won't do it, Noah," Doc said. "Billy, the assistant pro, will shoot 66 easily. Yeah, he wins every week; he is a plus-6 handicap at the club here." We went into the clubhouse to have a beer and hand in our scores. Sure enough, when I saw Billy's score, it was 64! I just played a great round of golf thinking I was on top, when in reality, I got destroyed. Little did I know he was only one of many who could shoot these low scores in Phoenix. The question I had was: If all these players were shooting so well, then why were they not competing on the pro tour?

I soon made friends with a bunch of the guys at the club and started playing in the money tournament every week. I was teaching a few lessons here and there but was more interested in working on my game and seeing how much I could progress. I decided to take a different approach with my teaching and recruitment of students. During my practice sessions, I had a three-foot-tall sign put up that said, "Does This Swing Look Effortless? Ask Me About Effortless Golf." People were constantly approaching me and asking me to explain. I would give them a short introduction to effortlessness and that was enough to whet their appetites and prompt them to ask about lessons. I was really hoping to find students to take golf schools, not so much lessons. Lessons are very tedious and, in my opinion, don't allow the student to progress as fast as they could. When a student is part of a school, they are constantly being pushed by the other students, forcing them to develop together. With individual lessons, the dichotomy is very different, being a one-on-one approach. The student is prone to initial discouragement, and often the progress is stalled. Unfortunately, I was only finding students who wanted hourly lessons. It was at that point that I decided I would focus more on my own game rather than promoting Effortless Golf. I signed up to play in one of the Gateway Tour events later that month. I practiced and played every day to prepare for the tournament. I enlisted Dave Inoshita, one of the guys I became friends with at the club, to be my caddie. Dave believed in my swing as much as I did. He was a scratch golfer who, to me, only seemed to be missing what I was always talking about—a clear, aware mind.

When we arrived for the tournament, I was confident in my abilities, and considering that I had shot 68 at this course the week before, I was very hopeful of a good outcome. My playing partner was Benoit Beisser, one of the contestants on the TV show "Big Break." Up to this point, I had seen a ton of golf played and felt I had a good idea what was needed to compete at the highest level.

On the first hole, I was out-driven by forty yards and saved par, while Benoit made birdie. In fact, he made eight birdies and an eagle on a course that had one of the highest slope ratings in the Phoenix valley, Troon North Golf Course. Benoit shot 65 and was in fifth place. That's right ... fifth! Four players shot lower, with the leader shooting a 62. It became clear I was out of my league, just like when I played the money tournament a few months back.

This tournament had a huge effect on me. I was more than two years into playing Effortless Golf but had not shot anything lower than a 69 in tournament competition. Were these players doing something different than I was? Would I ever shoot a 62? Maybe I'm just not good enough. I started to doubt myself as well as Effortless Golf.

I stayed in Phoenix for a few more months working on my game, but the more I practiced, the worse I seemed to be getting—just like when I was younger. I also saw that effortlessness was starting to become harder and harder to maintain. I was no longer doing all my actions in a state of love. I was really struggling. It seemed as though effortlessness was becoming a chore and not something that came naturally like before. I felt as if I was spinning my wheels and not making any real progress. People were also not flocking to my schools as I had hoped, so my money was running low.

Right as I was at my wit's end, I received a phone call from an old friend, Philip. He called to tell me that Cirque Du Soleil was looking for a prop master and wondered if I was interested. My answer was a resounding yes. The plan to allow love and effortlessness to direct my actions had failed, or so I thought. All I could seem to ask myself was, why? Why had this incredible insight led me down this path? Why was I unable to play at a high level and why was effortlessness no longer easy but now a chore? Before continuing with my golf game, I needed the answers to these questions. I left Phoenix with more questions than I had arrived with. I left knowing that unless my game took a huge leap forward, I would just be wasting my time and money playing in golf tournaments. My desire for teaching golf was also waning because of my own personal setbacks with the game. How could I be confident in anything I was teaching if I couldn't master the concepts myself? I knew I had no business teaching anyone until I had a firm understanding of my own approach.

CHAPTER 19

When an actor plays a scene exactly the way the director orders, it isn't acting. It's following instructions. Anyone with the physical qualifications can do that
– James Dean

I BEGAN WORK IN MONTREAL, Canada, the home of Cirque Du Soleil, on a new production called "Zarkana." It was to be the largest stage show to ever travel the world, and I was the new head prop master. We would be traveling to Orlando for pre-production then on to Radio City Music Hall in New York City, followed by Madrid and finally, Moscow. This job consumed all of my time over the next year, leaving me little time for golf and even less for effortlessness. I was no longer someone who talked and preached love; instead, I was someone focused on my career and all the trappings of life. When we finally arrived in New York, I was burned out. We had been working nonstop for more than eight months preparing and building this massive show; it was three times the size of anything I had done before.

Shortly after arriving in New York, I received a call from Ralph. I had not heard from him for quite some time, so this call was a little out of the blue. He started telling me how he had made some huge discoveries in his golf swing, and he

was going to send me a video so I could see it for myself. I was intrigued and couldn't wait to watch it. When the video arrived, I was very surprised by what I saw. Here was a guy, no taller than 5-feet-6, smashing the ball over 320 yards. His swing looked completely different from before. My only issue with his swing was its lack of flow. "Flow" was a word I had coined years ago to describe a golf swing that looked natural, not forced. Any swing that was made free of mechanics just had a different tempo. A swing unencumbered had flow and was smooth. A swing that was being guided by thought had no flow and looked mechanical. I pointed this out to Ralph, but he was only concerned with the numbers logged on the Trackman swing analyzer, and he certainly had those numbers, so maybe flow was overrated. When compared to the effortless swings, the difference was dramatic. Ralph looked totally different, and you could see all the parts of the body moving aggressively.

He told me that he had been studying the biomechanics of the swing for the past year and had met some amazing people in this field. One person he was convinced had the answers to his problems was a gentleman from Alaska named Kevin Mihoma. Kevin was a traditional teacher who became discouraged with his teaching method when he saw how the instruction he was giving wasn't improving his players—in fact, it was making them worse. As a result, Kevin set out on his own to see if he could find the reasons for this lack of improvement. He was convinced that the top players in the world were doing things that others weren't. In order to uncover this mystery, he took high-speed video and slowed the swing down to study it at the most microscopic level. By doing this, he was able to see that the top players in the world were making what Kevin called "invisi-moves." These moves could only been seen when video from a high-speed camera was played in slow motion. The top players were doing techniques at such a micro level that those movements could not be seen with the naked eye. But when you slowed the swings down on high-speed video, you could see these "invisi-moves." And then it all became clear.

All of these "invisi-moves" were showing him a sequence that only the top players in the world were doing. The only problem was that Kevin had no proof other than the video. He could not do the moves himself. Ralph decided the only way to prove Kevin's theory was to train himself by slowly and methodically making the movements over and over again. After a year, the results were certainly dramatic and did seem to work. Ralph felt that with the proper physical training and then the proper mental training, which we already had, maybe ... just maybe ... he could compete on a consistent basis with the best. I was interested and very intrigued.

The next few months were long and tiring. The show was up and running, and we would be leaving New York for Madrid. One night after work, as was my custom, I was riding my bike home to Brooklyn. It wasn't a terribly long ride, but that night the streets were wet from an earlier rain. As I made the turn onto my street, my foot slipped off the pedal and hit the ground. The bike fell to the side, trapping my ankle against the curb, and in an instant, my ankle snapped in three places. There would be no Madrid and no golf for me anytime in the near future. Luckily, no pins or surgery were required, but a long healing process would definitely be needed. This meant giving up my job traveling the world, but even so, I was not hugely disappointed. My real passion was golf, although now my future in the sport was uncertain. The injury happened the first week of June, which meant I probably wouldn't be playing any golf for the rest of the season. I was eager to try Ralph's new discovery, but it would have to wait.

My recovery was spent at my parents' house, where at least I had my mom and dad to help me. Thank God for a loving mother and father, who had always tried to be there for me.

A broken ankle is a very debilitating injury. I had broken my wrist a few years ago and managed just fine, but this was a real struggle. Luckily, my parents had a pool, which I used every day to strengthen my ankle during the recovery process. For the first month, I read and studied all the information that Ralph recommended. He shared Kevin's online work, and after a few weeks, the argument for what he was proposing began to make perfect sense. I was very cautious of adopting anyone's theories, though, because I had become all too aware of how theories and beliefs could be blinding.

I decided that once my leg healed, I would go back to Arkansas and visit Ralph. If I could see the swing live in action, I would know if this was the right thing for me. Finally, at the beginning of October, I made the trip down. My leg was healed, but my confidence in it wasn't. I was still afraid to put all my weight on my ankle because of the pain, or the anticipation of pain. I walked with a limp for the first month or so after the cast was off, and now I was in Arkansas attempting to make full golf swings. I wasn't totally sure if my leg would hold up, but now was the time to find out.

I arrived in Arkansas full of energy to learn something new. Ralph was excited to show me his swing, too. We went straight to the range, where he began hitting balls. The results were dramatic: He was hitting 8 irons 180 yards like it was nothing! Any club he hit was farther than any one I had seen before. It was truly something to behold. He told me that what he had learned was that you can train the body to move like this only if you learn in slow motion. Meaning, you stand in front of a mirror and go through small movements, making sure they are all in perfect sequence before you continue on to the next part of the swing. He essentially broke the swing into small pieces that you could slowly progress through. He did this with only a mirror and indefinite patience. No ball was used. Ralph showed me some of his students with whom he was working and how they had progressed to finally hitting a ball after a few weeks of the training. I could see by watching the videos that all of the students now had some of the same movements as the tour pros I watched on TV. He was developing tour-level moves in average-ability players, and I was impressed. My only issue was I still saw no flow in any of the swings, including Ralph's.

For the next three days, I worked on practicing these slow-motion drills with Ralph's watchful eye locked on my swing the whole time, correcting any mistakes I might be making. We would look at the video of my swing with the new movements, and sure enough, all the things I saw wrong with my swing—or what I thought were wrong with the swing—were disappearing right before my eyes. By the time I left, I felt I had a firm grasp of what I needed to do. These exercises, coupled with all the reading I had done over the past months, would surely have me hitting just like Ralph within a few months' time. I thanked Ralph for his instruction and returned to New York, ready to attack the game.

CHAPTER 20

Order cannot possibly be brought about through conformity to a pattern under any circumstance
– Jiddu Krishnamurti

When I returned home I began the rigorous training program that I thought was needed to push me onward and upward. After about a week, I started to question what I was doing. I took a step back and asked myself: How could I follow a swing that I could see had no flow? This swing, I was learning, would never truly be mine, because it would always be an imitation of someone else. It didn't feel natural. Here I was 39 years old, having spent the better part of five years following Gravity Golf and only reaching a certain level, then moving on to Effortless Golf, an approach that I devised but that still left me unsatisfied with the results. Was I about to do the same thing with Ralph's teaching?

Ralph's approach was that of imitation. Yes, from that imitation he yielded results, but I felt that if I followed this approach and tried to mirror a particular swing, then I wasn't being true to myself or my talents. Ralph would often cite a quote sometimes attributed to Picasso: "Good artists copy, great artists steal." This quote always bothered me and made me question the meaning of a real artist. I knew in my heart that if I was going to succeed, or ever be at peace with golf, it would need to be on my terms. I called Ralph and told him my concerns and why I would no longer be studying his methodology. He thought I was stubborn. Maybe I was, but something about all this just didn't ring true. I was reminded of a quote I had heard years earlier from the author Herman Melville: "It is better to fail in originality, than to succeed in imitation." For my whole life, when it came to golf, I have always followed that little voice that kept pushing me in a certain direction, and that voice was saying loud and clear that this was not the direction for me. I knew Ralph was disappointed, and I could tell he was a bit hurt with my decision. I told Ralph a story I had heard about a guy named Bob:

Bob was a high jumper in high school and was having a hard time competing at the highest level. He just couldn't jump as high as the other guys around the country. No matter how much he tried to copy and do what the best were doing, he still could not win an event. Then one day, he changed the entire sport by creating a paradigm shift in the way high jumping was done. He broke free of all the traditional ideas about how to jump over the bar. Instead of jumping forward, stomach first, as it had always been done, he decided to try to jump backward over the bar. With that one jump, he changed the sport forever. He eventually made it to the Olympics and won the gold medal. This new style of high jumping was coined the Fosbury Flop, named after Bob Fosbury. Every person in the sport had to learn how to jump like Bob or be left in the dust. He had stopped following others and found what worked for him. He found the freedom to challenge everyone, including himself.

My intention was to discover, on my own, what was the right swing for me. I had seen many players in Arizona shoot super low scores because they had great mechanics, but they were inconsistent and their careers never flourished. I was after something new, the unknown. The only thing Ralph's me-

chanics had to show me was what others were doing. I wanted to go beyond that.

CHAPTER 21

Man cannot discover new oceans unless he has the courage to lose sight of the shore
– André Gide

THE ONLY WAY I was going to find "my" swing was to go back to the basics and start fresh. The first thing I did was join a driving range so I could hit as many balls as possible, over and over again. I also signed up for a couple of tournaments to see if I could learn anything while playing under tournament pressure. My first tournament would be local qualifying for the U.S. Open in May, which was several months away, so I had time to train. I joined the only club close enough for me to get any use out of: Chelsea Piers in Manhattan, which also happened to be one of the best.

Chelsea Piers is a driving range that floats on an old pier in the Hudson River. It's four stories tall with 52 hitting stalls and automated tees that keep track of the balls you hit—all things that made joining a no-brainer for me. I was going to the range daily and trying every idea that popped into my head. This training went on for almost three months without any real tangible results. The Open was right around the corner, and I was running out of time. I decided that if I played poorly, so be it. There would be more tournaments down the road. Pressure and anxiety would only cloud my mind.

I had only four weeks before the U.S. Open local qualifier in Egg Harbor, New Jersey, at Hidden Creek Golf Club, a course designed by Ben Crenshaw and Bill Coore. I chose this particular course, because from what I could see of it online and having visited the area, I could expect a course similar to the Hot Springs Village tracks—wide open with somewhat rolling terrain. The real challenge would be the greens and short game.

During all this training, I was also able to land a job on the Broadway show "Jersey Boys" as an assistant prop master. The show had a great schedule, allowing me to get in plenty of practice, as well as supply me with enough money to pay for all these tournaments and my monthly bills.

After weeks of hitting balls every day, I wasn't improving as I had hoped. In fact, I wasn't improving at all. I seemed to be going in circles, hitting short, weak shots that to an average player looked great, but I knew better. They were far from great. But I was steadfast in my resolve to find my own approach and not imitate. After having tried so many different swings with nothing working out, I resorted back to Effortlessness. During my practice sessions at the range, I tried to be as effortless as possible, holding the club as gently as I could and trying to feel everything with complete awareness. But even with all this attention, my brain was still searching for an answer. I would make a great swing that would feel amazing and as soon as it was over, I would try to repeat the action and feeling. Then after about fifty swings or so, that great-feeling swing would mysteriously vanish just as it always had. The lack of consistency was driving me crazy!

Finally, the day before the tournament, I discovered what I consider to be the next piece in the puzzle to this mystery called the golf swing. I was at work all day on Broadway and didn't get to the range until later that night. Still, I had a good couple of hours to get some practice in before I called it a night. I arrived at the range befuddled. It was only a few months ago that I told Ralph his method was wrong, and here I was about to play in my favorite tournament all year with no possible chance of competing. Then right there at the range, I had a breakthrough moment. I remembered a few years back when I was with Ralph at the Monday qualifier in Dallas. After both of us failed to qualify, we went back to the hotel to have dinner and discuss our round. I had a few swing theories to show Ralph, so after dinner we went out to the parking lot to my car. I grabbed a 7 iron from the trunk, dropped a ball on the ground, and looking to an abandoned field in front of us, took a huge rip at the ball without any thought as to how to do it. I shanked the ball dead right, just barely missing the car next to us. "Why can't I just do that? Why can't I just swing the way my body and brain wants without me trying to control it?" I asked Ralph.

Ralph replied, "Because if you do, you will shank it just like that. You need to train the body." I was confused and frustrated. There had to be something more to this.

I didn't realize it then, but it was at that moment that I truly made a swing in freedom for the first time. I had always thought the day with Johnny was the real discovery, but the truth was, it was that night in Dallas. Now here I was, years later, realizing that the reason Effortlessness failed was because I had turned it into a method. I gave rules to the swing. I was telling people to stop using force and to hold the club gently, etc. What I was doing was developing a method, and a method implies structure. Freedom has no structure. I had been trying to play golf with no effort, when all along that defied true freedom, for freedom is the ability to move in all directions at once. And it was quite possible freedom wanted to use effort, but I never gave it a chance to try.

I now asked myself one simple question: What did I find that night in Dallas and that day with Johnny? I knew the answer. I had discovered freedom. Real freedom was not some effortless action; it was just freedom with no actual direction.

I thought the only action that was right was an action in love. This was a true statement, but I had decided what love was by moving and talking gently, holding the club gently. Real love was not something that could be practiced; it was something that came naturally. Yes, love was all of the things I was describing, but forcing it to happen was not allowing freedom or love to express itself fully. I realized that by forcing effortlessness, I was denying freedom.

I stood at the ball and said to myself, "Don't do anything! No gentleness, no love, no hate—just let go of everything!" I took my first swing and bam! A dead shank just like that night in the parking lot with Ralph. I swung again and again, only to hit more shanks. I shanked the ball continuously for the next 20 minutes. I started to laugh at how consistently I was at shanking it. I began to realize that my brain was learning and getting a real lesson about the shanks. As long as I didn't try and fix the swing consciously, maybe the brain would figure out the whole mechanics thing on its own. By the end of the evening, I was shanking it only every other shot instead of every shot. It was humbling to say the least. Here I was only twelve hours away from teeing off for the U.S. Open qualifying, and I was shanking it every other shot. The only strange thing about this was, I was not scared at all. I wasn't scared because I was now seeing that real freedom was not trying to control anything, including the outcome tomorrow.

CHAPTER 22

Doubt everything. Find your own light.
– Gautama Buddha

THE NEXT DAY, I arrived at the course about two hours before my tee time to see if the shanks were still in full force. As I walked to the range, I saw all the other pros warming up. I was acutely aware of the fact that not one swing on the range was being struck in freedom. Everyone there was using some level of control. I dumped my bucket of balls on the ground and was ready to go. The wind was howling straight in my face at about 15 to 20 mph. I took my first swing without a thought of effortlessness or anything else. The ball came off the ground about ten feet high, dead straight and solid. I was hitting a 9 iron, and this trajectory was a bit surprising because I never hit it that low. As I hit a few more shots with the same results, I became a little frustrated. Why was I hitting it so low? I tried another club and then another, all with the same result. I stepped back from the balls and had a seat on the bench behind me. As I sat watching the other players hit high shots, I wondered what I was doing wrong. Just then as I sat quietly, I felt the sand from one of the players' divots hit my face. He was about five yards away, but the wind was howling.

When the sand hit my face, everything fell in place. The reason my ball was going so low was because, in freedom, my brain was free to create the shot best needed for the situation. The wind was the issue. My brain, left in freedom, was creating the exact shot needed for ultimate control in these windy conditions.

What an incredible insight! Here I was angry that I was hitting the ball so low, when all along, the low ball was the exact shot needed. As I hit more balls, I could see that the mind was unconsciously gauging the wind and varying each shot a little to see the ball's reaction. This was true creativity without any control by me. After about twenty minutes, I decided to hit a few 3 irons. As soon as I struck my first 3 iron, I felt a strange sensation of pressure on my right pointer finger as the club started down in the swing. I felt it on the following swings, too. So what did I do? I started making sure I felt that feeling on every shot I took, and the results were amazing. I was hitting every shot thirty yards longer than I normally did and with a much better trajectory. I kept trying to make that pressure happen, and it worked. After about thirty perfect shots with my 3 iron, I stopped and said to myself, "What are you doing?!" I was falling into the same old trap. I would find something that seemed to work, and I kept trying to repeat it. I had done this all my life, and within a week or a month, I would dismiss it and find a new feeling to attach myself to, all of the time denying true freedom.

True freedom is what I felt when I first arrived at the course, the feeling of not knowing what was to come, the feeling of not holding on to any swing thought or idea. As I walked to the first tee, I told myself that I would not look for that finger pressure or any other temporary fix. Instead, I would allow freedom to operate, and if that meant shanking it all day, so be it. I would no longer influence my actions through conscience control in any way.

I met my caddie at the tee box, a young teenager named

Michael, who caddied at the course when he wasn't at school. I immediately said to him, "Hi Mike. I'm Noah, I don't hit it very far, I can't putt worth a damn, and I've been shanking pretty much all my shots for the last day." He looked at me in complete silence, unsure whether I was kidding him. "Yeah, just a heads-up—this could be a long day," I said to him.

I was greeted by a tournament official and introduced to my playing partners. I would be teeing off last in the group. As the other two players teed off, the official struck up a conversation with me about golf. We chatted until it was my turn to hit. This whole time, I was calm and relaxed. I walked up to the tee without any hesitation or thought of any kind. I stuck my peg in the ground and took a mighty rip. The ball soared high and far, just in the right rough about 290 yards off the tee. Not a bad shot, I thought. Certainly better than a shank.

The next shot was from the rough, an area of the game I always struggled with. I could only see about half of the ball, as it was sitting down in the heavy grass. I reached in the bag, pulled out an 8 iron, and without a thought about how to hit it, I knocked the ball eight feet from the pin. I think my caddie was as surprised as I was. I missed the putt but realized this might not go as bad as I expected. On the next drive, I asked how far it was to the bunker on the right. The caddie told me that it was 300 yards. Due to my Broadway work schedule, I was unable to play the practice round and get a feel for the course. As a result, I was playing the course blind, having never seen nor played it before this day. I took dead aim at the sand because the shot was into the wind and, on average, I was hitting the ball only about 280 yards at the range all spring. I hit the ball great, right on line. When we finally got to the fairway, the ball was nowhere to be found. I assumed it must have rolled into the bunker, but it was not there either. Then just as I was about to give up and go back to the tee, Michael said, "Here it is!" It was about five yards ahead of the bunker,

in the rough. I had just hit the ball into the wind over 300 yards. What was going on?

I hit the ball on the green about 20 feet from the stick. As Michael and I walked to the green, he said, "You're not that short of a hitter. I've only seen a few guys ever hit it farther than that on this hole." I laughed and told him that this was not my normal swing. Over the next few holes, I kept the score at even par. At the sixth hole, our first par-3, I was faced with a 180-yard shot to a two-tiered green that had a pin in the most inaccessible place, on the lower left tier. I stood on the tee box, aimed straight at the stick. But I knew that if I aimed where I wanted to, I would not hit a good shot. I backed away from the shot and said to myself, "I am confused. And if I am confused, then I am in no position to be making a decision."

I would allow my subconscious to make the decision for me. I would not aim the ball at all. I would just walk to the ball and trust that my subconscious would figure it out better than my conscious, confused mind could. I stood over the ball with my alignment nowhere near the flag—in fact, I was lined up toward the right side of the green on the upper tier, away from the pin. I took my swing, and the ball landed safely on the upper tier, maybe 40 feet from the flagstick. Both of my competitors hit it right at the stick, seemingly hitting great shots. We could not see their balls land because the green was hidden by a huge bunker fronting the green.

When we got to the green, both of their balls were missing. They had hit the green, and the balls bounced off the back into the rough. I had a brutal downhill putt that broke about ten feet to the right. Both of the other players couldn't control the spin coming out of the heavy rough and were left with tough putts to save par. My putt was so fast and hard to read that I felt the only chance I had was to take the same approach with the putting as I did with the tee shot—let the subconscious take over and sort it out. I approached the putt with no line in mind. My putter seemed to move on its own and then the ball was gone. When I first hit it I thought, "That's going to be at least 12 feet past the hole," but the more it went down the hill, the more it looked like it might be a great putt and even go in. The putt went right to the edge of the cup and just missed, sliding about three feet past.

Both of the other players missed their putts and made bogeys. I stood over my three-foot putt and saw about six inches of break on a very slick green. I trusted in my subconscious and stepped up to the putt, hitting the ball dead straight and with enough power to hit it ten feet past if I missed. It dropped dead center in the hole. A small clap came from the hill just above the green. As I walked up the hill, I was met by my admirer. The man clapping was a rules official watching the action. He congratulated me on making par, saying it was one of only a few all day on that particular hole. It was an amazing feeling but also had me questioning everything I had ever learned about golf.

Until that point in my career, I had always assumed the only way to play golf was through analyzing the course. I had realized earlier that day that conscious control of the swing wasn't necessarily needed. But this was taking things to a whole new level. I was now allowing the subconscious to guide me and choose my shots. I was realizing that any conscious control at all was limiting my ability to play my best.

I finished the front nine at 1-over par and missed a few putts that could have put me under par. The back nine was more of the same. I just trusted in the subconscious and its ability to perform. It felt much the same way that it does when you play catch with a friend. You don't think about mechanics—you just throw the baseball where you are looking. I started to realize that this is how touch is developed. I could throw a ball to someone with speed or as gentle as I wanted and no real thought was required. I had always wondered how tour golfers could be so delicate with tough shots around the

green. I was always thinking of my mechanics, which left me unable to feel any touch. Now I was chipping it close every time I missed a green.

This round was going great, but if I was going to qualify, I needed to step up my game. By the time I reached the sixteenth hole, I could sense that I would need to be under par to qualify, and I was currently 3-over. Normally, I would press and try to make birdies. Not today. It was very clear to me that there was nothing mentally nor physically I could do that would help my case. I was resigned to accepting the outcome, and I wasn't going to consciously do anything. My drive on the sixteenth was dead center in the fairway, followed by a 7 iron that landed thirty feet short of the pin. When I walked up to the putt, I felt like the ball was going to go in before I even hit it. Sure enough, it never left the cup, only to hit the back edge and bounce out. I let out a big sigh; it was such a good putt. On the par-5 seventeenth, I hit a good drive about 250 yards out. Now, I knew I needed an eagle, but when I went to the bag, my eyes looked right at my 7 iron, not the 3 wood that I thought I needed and made sense. It was the hardest thing in the world to do, but I went with the 7 iron. I was "all in" with the subconscious, and choosing the 3 wood would have gone against that.

I had no idea how all this was working, but somehow it was. Sure enough, I hit the 7 iron dead center, then a wedge to twelve feet, but finished with the same result as the last hole, another lip-out. As we walked off the green, my caddie apologized, saying it was his fault that I missed. "You have been hitting all your putts exactly where I've directed you, and I've been reading the putts all wrong." I told him it wasn't his fault at all and that this was the game of golf—if I'm hitting the hole, I can't ask for much more. Little did he know, I wasn't even trying to aim where he wanted. I was just lining up wherever my body and brain wanted.

On eighteen, I hit my best drive of the day, straight into a howling wind to a crowned fairway with trouble on both sides. I had 160 yards left to the flagstick and as I looked at the green, the shot to the pin looked relatively straightforward. Michael informed me that the pin was a sucker placement. The hole was actually sitting directly on a ledge with a ten-foot false front. This was valuable information, to say the least. As I walked to my bag, my eyes locked on my 6 iron. This was way too much club for the shot, but I took it without hesitation. I made what I felt was a normal swing, but the shot went super low, and when it hit the green, it landed right into the false front, took one huge bounce, and landed eight feet from the hole. Any less club and the ball would have hit that same spot and rolled down the false front. How was my brain doing this? How was my subconscious figuring out all these creative shots without me even trying?

True to form, I missed the putt with another lip-out. I had just lipped out the final three birdie putts of the day, but I saw the silver lining: I was playing my best and hitting amazing shots. I wasn't choking under pressure. If I started working on my putting, maybe those putts would eventually drop. I walked to the scoring tent to see my final results, and sure enough, I had missed by one shot. There were still forty players left to come in, so I knew I would be missing by more than one shot in the end. To my surprise, I ended up finishing in a tie for fourteenth, only two shots away from qualifying. The scoring average for that day was 78.9. The wind wreaked havoc with most of the players. I, however, never even noticed it.

I left the course with a sense of the unknown, and that to me was more rewarding than qualifying. I had always known that freedom was the key to reaching my full potential, and now I was playing in that freedom. I couldn't wait to get home and start working on this new-found approach and see where the unknown would take me.

I arrived back home and received a call from Ralph, who

congratulated me. He felt this was an impressive accomplishment, considering I had broken my ankle less than a year before and had not been playing in any golf tournaments. I thanked him and tried explaining what I had found—my insight into the subconscious—but he was not interested in hearing it. At first, I was a bit taken aback by Ralph's closed-mindedness but then realized that trying to convince others was not my goal. I was actually beginning to see that all I wanted to do was play golf in freedom and see where it would lead me. This was my own journey. Maybe I had just created my own Fosbury Flop. For the first time in years, I was confident I was headed in the right direction.

CHAPTER 23

Creativity is more than just being different. Anybody can plan weird; that's easy. What's hard is to be as simple as Bach. Make the simple, awesomely simple, that's creativity
– Charles Mingus

WHEN I GOT BACK to the range, I started hitting shots with this new mindset. Instead of trying to repeat a swing, I was free to swing in any fashion my brain chose. In fact, "chose" is the wrong word. Choice implied confusion, and I was not confused. I would allow my mind to swing with any tempo, any shape, and any stance it wanted, and believe me, it did. This was like handing a kid a paintbrush and saying "have at it." I started to see the course and range as my canvas, and the clubs were my brushes, with the ball being the paint. This would be like when I first discovered Effortlessness and painted those pictures, except now, I would not be trying to be effortless. I would allow myself total freedom of movement. I realized that most golf practice was done at a target, which was also not freedom. The range was a place to allow freedom to truly express itself. It was a place of learning and experimentation. I had always approached the range as I think most people had, as a place to try to hone a certain feel and

movement, then carry that movement to the course. I would expect a certain result at the range, as well as on the course, and when that expectation wasn't met, I would get frustrated.

There are no bad shots in true freedom. Every shot is its own expression, much in the same way that learning to walk has no bad steps. The problem I saw was that no one was comfortable failing. Failing is essential in learning any skill. How else do we know what success is? I stopped aiming at targets on the range and, instead, started allowing my body and brain to hit the ball anywhere it wanted. I started hitting all kinds of amazing shots that I had no idea I was capable of. I was really seeing just how much I had been slowing my own development by adhering to other methods and mechanics.

Before, any shot that went dead left or right, I would try to analyze and correct. Now, I was accepting my shots, good or bad, without questioning them. This was all part of the learning process. This was the brain's way of learning its boundaries and limitations. Slowly, I was un-conditioning myself from all the years of belief about how to learn a golf swing. I felt like a small child, and I truly loved seeing what I would create from day to day. Some days, I would hit the ball high, then shanks, then low. Every day the swing was completely different because I was never trying to repeat anything from the day before; I never let myself lock onto any type of repetition. I would acknowledge that certain feelings produced certain results, but I would never try to repeat them. I know you must be thinking this is crazy, as this contradicts everything we have been taught. But if you open your mind to what I am saying and see the real freedom and creativity this brings, you might begin to accept that this does indeed work.

This leap of faith was nothing more than me being willing to let go of the beliefs about how the game should be approached. I was discovering for myself just how creative I could be. It definitely took some time for me to truly trust. I spent weeks hitting really bad shots, but I kept telling myself that a child falls hundreds of times when first learning to walk. The child never analyzes his falls; he just keeps trying until eventually he learns to walk without falling. This was the real key to learning—forgo the analyzing and allow the subconscious to work things out.

After a few weeks of practice, I wanted to get out on the course and experiment. My focus on the course was to watch and listen to my mind, to see if it was a conscious participant or if my mind was quiet, allowing the subconscious to operate in freedom. I learned very quickly that I analyzed everything—the wind, the distance, the club selection. Everything and anything was part of my mental chatter on the course. I started to approach the course in a whole new way: I would stand back on the tee and just observe what was in front of me. I would not exclude anything. I wanted to see it all. It felt as if during my whole golf career, I had been looking at the course through a straw, only seeing a very limited view. Now, with an open mind and my subconscious guiding me, I was able to see the whole picture and absorb every detail of the course.

With this sense of freedom and clear view of the course, I began walking to the bag and selecting the first club my eyes focused on. This feeling of "locking on" was a total state of intelligence and lacked any confusion. Once more, my mind would view the clear vision of the course as I walked into the ball and swung. There would be no aiming or conscience point of direction, just a sense of trust and freedom that my mind would figure all this out without my conscious input. Where should I aim? How should I swing? I left everything to the subconscious.

Now I know what you are saying—what if I walked to the bag and pulled a wedge on the tee of a par-5? The simple answer is: If that's where my subconscious led me and where my eyes found their focus, then I would pull that wedge. But what I found was that never happened. In freedom, the mind

is no longer operating in confusion; it is operating in supreme order. When you analyze everything, you are dealing with limited information. You can only think consciously about so many things before you need to hit the ball. By not analyzing, I was seeing everything at once and, therefore, was no longer limited and confused.

My mind always seemed to choose the proper club, and on the rare occasions when I hit a bad shot on the course, I realized that I had consciously interfered on some level. You need to be acutely alert and honest with yourself about this. Paying attention is the only thing required for learning, and most of the time, we are overthinking, not paying close attention.

Another interesting phenomenon I experienced was when I quieted my mind and felt completely at peace, yet still hit what I thought was a bad shot. Much to my surprise and delight, on the next shot I usually ended up chipping in or knocking it stiff. It was almost as if the brain was creating its own way of completing the task instead of the way I thought it should go. I started having total peace with every shot I hit on the course, and as a result, within days my scores started dropping. I was learning to trust my subconscious, and that trust resulted in a creativity I had not yet imagined. I came to the conclusion that I needed to dedicate some real time to this approach. It was unlike anything I had ever encountered, and it needed awareness and understanding to be mastered. I decided to spend one full year training and playing in this manner to see what freedom and creativity could do if left to operate on their own.

CHAPTER 24

The function of the creative artist consists of making laws, not in following laws already made
– Ferruccio Busoni

THE FOLLOWING WEEKEND I headed upstate to practice some shots at the Monster golf course. It was good to get away from the range where I could only hit from mats, and onto a course. I wanted to try a variety of shots—out of the heavy rough, on side-hill lies, maybe a few bunker shots. My girlfriend, Jennifer, who had never played golf, and my fifteen-year-old nephew, Joshua, who was also a golf neophyte, decided to tag along. Up until then, Josh had shown very little interest in golf, so I was excited when he said he would come along.

When I pulled up to the first tee, my eyes instantly focused on the driver. I then walked to the back tees. At 7,650 yards, this course earns its name as the Monster. I wasted no time in hitting a drive dead pure right down the middle. This first hole was a long par-5, so unless you kill it off the tee, it's most likely a three-shot hole. My second shot was a five wood about fifty yards short of the green. My third shot was a clean wedge that rolled about twenty feet past the cup, just on the fringe. Jennifer complimented me on the shot, but I knew I

had missed an opportunity to get a gimme birdie.

My nephew Josh joined me on the green to learn how to caddie. I asked him to read the putt, explaining to him how most putts are read by how far in or outside the cup the ball will break, or move. He told me one cup to my left. What I didn't tell him was that I gave up that form of reading putts a month ago. I addressed my putt and with total clarity struck the ball. It rolled nicely, and in a flash, it was in the hole. I started with a birdie. What a way to start! My girlfriend, almost surprised, said, "You made it!"

I said, "Of course!" as if I always make twenty-foot birdie putts.

The next hole was a par-4 and I hit two great shots. Unfortunately, the second shot wasn't quite far enough, which left me with a long chip. I hit it to four feet and made the downhill putt. The same thing happened on the next hole, only this time I chipped it to one foot for an easy tap-in. The next hole was the No. 1 handicap hole, a very long par-5 that measured 636 yards. I had about seventy yards left for my pitch after two great shots. This distance has always been an issue for me. I usually blow an easy birdie attempt with a poor pitch. Not this time. I hit the ball to two feet and tapped in for birdie. The next two holes were routine pars with nothing much surprising happening. On the seventh hole, however, I blistered a 5 wood to a 250-yard uphill par-3. I was about thirty feet from the hole. With my putter in hand and a clear mind, I struck the ball. It felt a little short, but to my surprise, it just kept tracking and finally rolled into the hole.

Right after this putt, I knew something was different. I hadn't played or putted this well in a very long time. I was in the zone. As soon as I walked off the green, I told Jennifer, "I'm in the zone. You are seeing something special today." I parred the next two holes leaving me 3-under for the front nine, my lowest round on that side ever. As I walked to the tenth tee, I was acutely aware of how easy and natural the game of golf was for me that day.

In fact, the only hard part was staying out of the way. I hit two perfect shots to the green but proceeded to three-putt. I realized this was the only time I questioned my read on the green, and in that moment of hesitation, my mind was not able to be fully aware. I hit the putt short and missed the 5-footer. From that point on, I just put the game on cruise control and trusted my subconscious completely.

On the next hole, I hit the ball to ten feet and on the following hole, the par-5 twelfth, I hit it to twelve feet for eagle. I missed my eagle, but I gained so much insight into how the swing worked best. It works best when we stay out of the way consciously and allow our creative mind to operate in freedom. Next, we pulled up to the thirteenth, a short par-4 at 360 yards that plays even shorter if you take the ball over the trees. The hole was a dogleg right with about a 265-yard carry over the trees. I could usually carry the trees, but it was another thirty yards to the green. Most of the time, I would just have a little flip wedge to the green. This time was different, though. As I put my tee in the ground and stood back to hit, I noticed that I was looking at a different part of the hole. I was staring at the right side of the green. I usually lined up to the left side, which was a shorter carry over the trees. This time I found myself standing and aligning myself in a whole new way. I said to Jen, "I've never done this before," and then bam! I hit the shot, a towering drive about ten yards to the right of my normal line. I hit it really well, but it was headed straight at the bunker guarding the right side of the green. I looked through the trees and thought I saw a ball bounce on the green, but from that distance, it was hard to be certain. When we arrived at the green, I realized my eyes were not deceived; I had actually reached the surface of the green! What a day I was having. The putt for eagle was about thirty-five feet uphill with a strong break to the right. I struck my putt, and it curved away from the hole by about five feet. I missed the putt

for birdie and left with a par. The first time in my life that I reached the green in one shot, and I ended with a three-putt. As you can imagine, this was more than disappointing.

The fourteenth, a 185-yard par-3, is the easiest hole on the course. The last few times I played here, I came close to a hole-in-one but could never quite get it in. Now I would have another chance. When my eyes locked on my 8 iron, I was a little surprised since this was a long way for me to be hitting with an 8 iron. I usually hit my 8 about 155 yards, but this was the club I reached for. Trusting the subconscious to guide me. I told Jen that maybe today was my day for a hole-in-one, especially since I was playing so well and everything seemed to be going in my favor. My chances were definitely better than normal. The elusive shot I had been looking for ever since my unofficial ace all those years ago in Arkansas, was right in front of me. Some players get five or ten holes-in-one in a lifetime. I had only one, and that wasn't even during a real round of golf.

I struck the ball, and as soon as it left the tee, it was like it was attached to the flagstick. "Go in the hole!" I said aloud, and sure enough, the ball hit the stick and dropped straight down about five feet away. Close, but no cigar. I was so frustrated about not getting the hole-in-one that I missed the five-foot putt—another shot given away after my mind started wandering. I parred the next two holes bringing me to the seventeenth at 4-under. The seventeenth at the Monster is what I consider to be the best risk-reward hole I have yet to see. It plays 435 yards. The tee shot can be played in two different ways. You can lay up to the right to an island-type fairway that runs out at 220 yards into a pond, with water on the left and right of the landing area. The other option is to bomb it left over the lake, which is a carry of about 250 yards. The fairway over the carry is only about 25 yards wide, and water awaits any shot that goes a little bit right. If you lay up, you will have a 200-yard shot minimum, but if you go for it, you're left with a little flip wedge to the green.

As I stood on the tee with my driver, I felt a sense of fear come over me. My mind was riddled with confusion: I'm 4-under ... maybe I should just lay up. I would hate to blow this round. Right then I saw how thought was trying to sabotage the round. This was the same thought process I had that day back in the Monday qualifier in upstate New York when I was 5-under. I put my mind at ease and reminded myself that I had hit almost every shot perfect today, so why would this drive be any different? I took a full rip and watched the ball sail dead center over the water and land safely on the other side. I hit the ball perfectly. I ended up making par and another one on eighteen, which left me with a 68. The course record, which had stood for about forty years, was 67. I came that close. I told Jen that because of her lack of golf knowledge, she truly couldn't appreciate what she had just seen. She told me she did appreciate it and said I made it look so easy and effortless. This made me smile. I might have not practiced all those shots out of the rough that I originally intended to that day, but this round of golf was something to behold.

CHAPTER 25

A person who never made a mistake, never tried anything new
– Albert Einstein

I WAS NOW READY to play in a few more tournaments. I did some research and signed up for the Maine State Open and the New Hampshire State Open. Both tournaments would be two-day events in the same week, with Maine on Monday and Tuesday, then New Hampshire on Wednesday and Thursday.

When I arrived in Maine, the weather was not cooperating; it was a torrential rainstorm. The course I would be playing at was named Augusta Country Club. My tee time on the first day was scheduled for 2:03 p.m., and I would be in the last group off. I pulled into the parking lot just as the rain was starting to subside. As I started to unload my clubs, I heard one of the players say the tournament had been canceled due to the weather. I immediately went into the clubhouse to get confirmation and was told that because the course was too wet for play, the tournament would be turned into a one-day shootout. We would be teeing off at the same times the following day. To get some practice and keep fresh, I headed to the range and putting green. The moment I started hitting balls, everything went wrong. I was back to shanking the ball, making poor contact and just hitting it really bad. After about a half-hour and no improvement, I decided to just head to the practice green. The result was the same; I was duffing chips and had no touch with the putter. This was really frustrating, considering how well I played just weeks before at the Monster. I left the course dejected, but I also knew my game could turn on a dime, and tomorrow was all that really mattered, not this practice session. I found a small hotel and had a nice dinner before heading to bed.

The next day was perfect weather with temperatures in the mid 70s and wind at around 5 mph, ideal conditions for a tournament. As I made my way to the range, I felt a true sense of fear come over me. I was terrified of playing poorly and began thinking about how this would be such a waste of a trip if I didn't finish well. I dumped my bucket of balls and took a swing. Shank! I was starting to think this was going to be the longest day of my life. Instead of trying to figure out the cause of these shanks, I decided to just accept it. I had been looking for the cause for a while now, and surely five minutes before teeing off wasn't the time for further analyzing. Instead, I resolved to just observe my swing—meaning, I would simply allow my swing to operate as usual and would watch it and feel it without trying to find a reason for the shank. Maybe looking for the cause was the very thing hindering me. I was also aware that this understanding was new, and the shanks were probably just part of the growing pains. If I could embrace this as part of the learning process, then with patience and practice my mechanics would improve. As I allowed myself to just observe my range session, I started noticing how my club was not soled flat on the ground; it was leaning forward, hooding the ball. I had never noticed this before, as my attention was always on the swing and not the setup.

By not questioning anything in my swing, I immediately began seeing all the different facets of my game. I saw and felt my posture and how my back was slightly rounded. I felt and

saw how strong my grip was, and I could feel how my eyes were locked on the ball. Instead of evaluating and analyzing these things or comparing them to other pro golfers, I just allowed myself to simply observe them. I never once labeled my posture, grip or any aspect of my game as "right" or "wrong." My body was moving and playing in its natural state, and I would not interfere with that. The more I watched and felt all these movements, the smoother my swing became, and in only a few swings, I was puring all my shots. I realized that I was reaching another level of awareness and freedom.

As I left the range and headed to the first tee that day, I knew it was important for me to watch how my swing worked, not how I thought it should work. My first tee shot was a great drive down the fairway, leaving me about 125 yards to the hole. I took a wedge and just observed the whole process from beginning to end, and by the time my observation was over, the ball was five feet from the pin. I missed the putt on the low side, which frustrated me a little. Over the next four holes, I just watched the swing, never criticizing, just observing. I was hitting shot after shot right at the pins. On the sixth hole, a par-3 measuring 185 yards, I hit a solid 6 iron that never left the stick. For a moment, I thought I was going to have my first official hole-in-one, but instead, it rolled over the cup, leaving me about two feet away.

I approached the short tap-in putt and felt a sense of fear, coupled with doubt. I had zero confidence I could make that putt, and sure enough, I made a terrible stroke and didn't even hit the hole. How could my swing be working so well and my putting be so bad? I had no answers, so I just kept plugging along, reminding myself that I needed to relax, observe, and learn. On the seventh hole, I finally made a birdie putt from about ten feet, which felt like a blind squirrel finding a nut in the woods, but I took it gladly. On the eighth hole, a short par-3, I had about twelve feet for birdie, and with the help of the golf gods, I made it, bringing me to minus-2. I felt like I should be 3- or 4-under at this point, but my poor putting was hurting my game. The ninth hole was a par-5 dogleg. I hit a perfect drive and was left in prime position to reach the green in two shots. My eyes locked on the bag, and without hesitation, I pulled a 5 wood. With all the confidence in the world, I hit the ball and watched as it sailed perfectly onto the green, leaving me with a 30-foot eagle putt. Unfortunately, my struggle with putting continued, and I missed the shot. But I was able to salvage a birdie for a 3-under 32 on the front side.

Heading to the back nine, I felt encouraged about my playing, even though the putting was lacking. On No. 10, I hit a great drive down the left side of the fairway and then stuck a wedge to about six feet for birdie. My putting wasn't improving and by the time I reached the fourteenth hole, I had missed three short putts on the back, but I was still 3-under. As I approached the tee on fourteen, one of the rules officials asked for my score. When I told him, his eyebrows raised and he said, "Well you're the only guy left with a chance to win."

Instantly, I felt excited. I was playing great and just needed to make a few good putts. Based on my putting performance so far, that was easier said than done. I told myself that this was what I had wanted all my life, to have a chance at winning a tournament. In that moment, I doubted my subconscious. I looked down the fairway and began questioning my club selection. Initially, my eyes had focused on the driver, but looking down the fairway, I could see the hazard running across it at about 270 yards. This was a long par-5 and my chance of reaching it in two seemed slim. I walked back to the bag and decided against the driver, grabbing the 3 wood instead to lay up. All day I had not questioned my club selection and had total trust in my subconscious. In that moment of doubt, I chose poorly.

I hit the 3 wood straight down the middle, leaving myself well over 300 yards to the green. I approached my fairway

shot and saw the ball sitting on a small bump. It looked as though a cereal bowl was tucked under the turf upside down and my ball came to rest on the downward edge of the bowl. I was in a position I had never seen before in all my years playing golf. I was totally confused. What should I hit? I still had a hazard right in front of me and needed about 60 yards to carry it. I pulled a 5 wood and took a rip. Sure enough, the club bounced into the ball, sending it sailing right about head-high over the hazard. It landed in the heavy rough, safely on the other side of the hazard. As I approached my ball, I realized this was my first shot out of the rough all day. I could barely see the ball, and to make things worse, I was totally out of my mental game. I was no longer trusting my subconscious to guide me, but instead, I was thinking and questioning how I was going to hit this ball out of the thickest rough I had ever seen. I hit an 8 iron head high out of the rough and straight at the bunker in front of the green. By the time I finally got the ball on the green and three-putted, I walked away with a 7.

As I walked to the next tee, I realized once again I had not learned to trust my subconscious. I recognized why I scored a 7, and it wasn't because my swing fell apart; it was because my mind fell apart. I immediately regrouped. I hit a driver on the next hole dead center and then hit a 9 iron to one inch from the hole for a disappointing birdie-3. I finished my round and carded a 69, well off the lead of 62. I was all too aware that my putting had kept me from a lower score, which I knew I was more than capable of shooting. Still, I was able to finish in a tie for twentieth place out of 156 competitors, which left me feeling like this new understanding of trusting the subconscious was truly capable of great things.

That night, I hopped in my car and drove the three hours to New Hampshire for the next event. The following day, I arrived at Owl's Nest Resort, a golf course totally different from Augusta. This track was a mountain course and total target golf. I would need to hit some really fine shots if I was going to have any chance of making the first-day cut of the top 50 players. That day, I had one of my greatest ball-striking days ever. I hit all but one fairway and only missed two greens. The problem, once again, was my putting. I shot a 77 and had 38 putts. The average tour player has 30 putts per round. I was so far off average, I couldn't believe it. I missed the cut and left New Hampshire shaking my head. I needed to understand why I was putting so poorly.

CHAPTER 26

A mind is like a parachute. It doesn't work if it's not open
– Frank Zappa

THE NEXT FEW MONTHS, I spent countless hours practicing my new understanding of trusting the subconscious. In that time, I convinced two players, Preston Truman Boyd and Douglas Jones, to join me in the training. One day, Preston and I played at Great Gorge Club in northern New Jersey, originally the Playboy Club back in the 1980s. The hotel had long since closed, but the course did a great job of evoking the feeling of a bygone era. The countertop at the grill was covered in old Playboy magazines, and the front of the golf carts had pictures of Playboy bunnies on them. All around the course and clubhouse were other details that gave this establishment a nostalgic feel, even down to the greens mower, which was straight from the 1970s. The course was a little rough around the edges but not the worst by any means.

This round at Great Gorge was one I was very much looking forward to, especially after my admirable finish in Maine and New Hampshire, notwithstanding my putting woes. It had been ten years since I last played Great Gorge, and I had forgotten most of the holes. The course was in a style similar to a Donald Ross design, with various elevated greens and turtle backs. The round was not spectacular at all but manageable. I shot 74 with 31 putts. Preston, on the other hand, was all over the map. By the fourteenth hole, he was done. Mentally, he had quit. I knew this was a very important time in his training. When we got to the No. 15, he pulled his drive some thirty yards left in the woods, so I instructed him to re-tee and try again. Once again, the ball went left into the woods. He tried again ... same result. This was perplexing to me because if the mind is free, it becomes very hard to repeat the same mistake over and over again. He must have been doing something mentally that was causing this problem.

On his next shot from the fairway, I asked Preston to talk out loud about what he was thinking. He walked me through how he was looking down the fairway at the green. He was thinking, "It's a hard wedge." There it was! He was consciously telling himself that he should swing hard. By doing this, he was consciously forcing his body to do something, which meant the mind was not free to operate and swing at its own pace. The mind is a very cunning thing when it comes to participation. It has a terrible time allowing the subconscious to operate. Once Preston was free from this, he striped the next shot right next to the flagstick. Then on the next hole, his drive was within ten yards of mine! This was a real boost for his confidence. After the round, Preston told me that those last few shots of the round were the best he's ever played and that it made the day. This made me feel great, as well, for it gave further validation to my teachings. Sometimes the reward is not always in the score.

Douglas, on the other hand, was seemingly making much smaller strides. He was having some difficulty with his swing and as much as I wanted to interject and help, I left it alone, hoping the necessary change would occur on its own. In that manner, the brain will learn on its own accord, instead of taking direction and simply following blindly. But in order

for this approach to work, you must have a free mind, and Douglas was not in a state of freedom. He was mechanically trying to control the action.

One day, Douglas approached me with some concern about his swing. He told me he could see (on video) and feel that he was a much better golfer than he was expressing on the course. His frustration and impatience were evident. He said he had been incorporating mechanics into his practice sessions. It was "easier" that way. He went on to explain that he was working on mechanics at the range and then harnessing the subconscious only while on the course. His argument was that if he could see a problem, why not fix it then, instead of waiting for the mind to sort it out? This was essentially the same conversation I had with Ralph just months earlier. The leap of faith I have taken to teach people how to trust themselves and their subconscious—fully, entirely, completely—had certainly had its challenges. But as we all know, anything worth doing is going to be a challenge.

I pondered Douglas' question and tried to help him understand what I was attempting to accomplish with this teaching. Douglas had only been playing golf for about two years when we first met. I had been working with him on his swing for roughly two months in total when he approached me with his worries. I explained to him that I had been studying the golf swing for sixteen years as a pro and another twenty years on top of that as a player. I did not come to my understanding of the swing, nor learn to play at this level, overnight. My swing and clarity on the golf course is the visible manifestation of years of preparation, both mental and physical. It involved countless hours and years of study, honing my craft both on the course and at the driving range.

Even now, I was still continuing to grow and learn as a player. I had been steadily improving over the past few months in ways I never expected. The only problem area that persisted was putting, and occasionally shanking the ball. Putting is half the game, so no matter how far and pure you strike the ball, you still have to get the flat stick rolling if you are ever going to score low. Putting should have been the easiest part of this development, but for me, that hadn't been the case. I always had a decent touch around the greens, but I have never considered myself a great putter. In my last tournament, I hit 93 percent of my fairways and 87 percent of greens in regulation. I shot a 77 and had 38 putts. Most tour pros average 29 to 30 putts per round. It was painfully obvious that the only part of my game not improving at the same rate was my putting.

I knew that a mechanical solution was not the answer, so I resorted to focusing more on the actions I was taking during the stroke, watching how my body parts moved, thinking this would surely help me. After hours on the putting green and no real sign of improvement, I returned to hitting full shots at the range. At about 100 swings in, the dreaded shank showed up. This time, though, I was intently alert and watching as closely as possible. Right then, I saw the cause of my problem. During my time with Cirque Du Soleil, one of my responsibilities was to inflate the airbag for the tightrope walkers. Every night, I watched these tightrope walkers from below, and the one thing I noticed was that they never looked down. They always looked straight ahead. This meant they were trusting in both their training and subconscious to guide them. I would now use this same approach in my golf swing. I decided that instead of focusing on the body's movements during the golf swing, I should be putting my attention on the clubhead. Just as the tightrope walkers' vision went beyond the wire, so would my focus go beyond the body.

On my first swing, with all my attention on the weight and movement of the clubhead and nothing else, I ended up hitting it dead center on the clubface. I began hitting shot after shot perfectly. Why was the action of bringing attention to the clubhead causing the shank to disappear? I knew I needed to hit some putts and see if that improved as well. Sure enough,

the putter was rock solid. I was not influencing the swing. In fact, all I was doing was feeling the action of the clubhead during the swing. The more I practiced this with every shot, the more it seemed like I had finally found the glue that held the swing together.

This was not something mechanical; it was just the opposite. By solely focusing on the clubhead, the rest of my body was allowed to move in complete freedom, without my own judgmental prying eye. The subconscious was now truly in control.

I tried to help Douglas understand how mechanics were limited and he would never reach his full potential by using them, but it was to no avail. He could not free his mind and accept that you have to allow yourself to fail before real growth can begin. He told me he tried my way and that he was getting worse, not better. I explained that the brain needs time to sort out all the moving parts. It won't happen overnight, I told him, but in the end, this understanding will lead you to your full potential as a golfer much quicker than not. You must trust in the process. Douglas' main argument was that I had already been taught mechanics, and as a result, mine were solid to begin with. All I was doing was allowing good mechanics to operate, he said. I asked him if he thought babies who were learning to walk had great mechanics already. The answer is, of course, no. And they certainly don't think about the mechanics involved. Children at that age can barely speak. Their minds are open and pliable, not filled with concepts and ideas. "Infancy conforms to nobody," as Emerson once so fittingly said. A child learning to walk does so on his own accord, with no understanding of the process, except that from observation. After multiple failed attempts and falls, they "figure it out." Soon, the child's subconscious mind realizes how to use all the muscles to do what he or she sees everyone else doing. It's that simple. This to me was enough proof to realize that you don't need conscious control to learn the golf swing—just the opposite. The swing needs freedom, and a quiet mind is freedom.

Douglas was not convinced; he decided to strike out on his own and figure it out for himself. I called Preston to get his take on Douglas and why he thought this was so hard for Douglas to accept. Preston had some insight: "Obviously if you 'work' on this method, it's not going to work. The total surrender to the method is the only way any improvement will work its way into the game. Douglas is still playing for a number. I have given in to not caring if I shoot an 80, 84, or 74. I used to golf every round with a number in my head. That's not how I want to golf anymore. I used to get angry and disappointed if I didn't break 80. I have now accepted the process and know the numbers will work themselves out. When I was younger, shooting mid to low 70s, I was making tons of pars. This past Wednesday, I made four birdies and a few bogeys, which to me, is much more interesting and artistic. The simplest way to describe this method is the walking analogy; you can't deny the fact that a toddler isn't using mechanics to get up and walk to a shiny bright toy at the other side of the room."

I could tell just by his response that Preston understood my teaching and was feeling the same freedom I had felt. I did question him on calling this a "method," as a method implies a structure to follow, and my teaching advocated anything but structure. We've already determined that methods don't work in the long run. The body changes over time and to use a method means using a sequence of movements that is the same day after day. The one constant in life is change, so to have a swing that never changes is ignorant of that fact. My teaching is not a method. It is an understanding, one that leads to the freeing of the mind and the subconscious. To answer the question of what was hindering Douglas from truly breaking through, I was left with only one conclusion—a closed mind is the hardest door to open.

CHAPTER 27

We live at the edge of the miraculous
– Henry Miller

THE TOURNAMENT SEASON was coming to an end and the final tournament of the year was the Van Cortlandt club championship. It was an honor to play at this distinguished course. Van Cortlandt, located in the Bronx, is the oldest public golf course in America and is steeped in history. This was a match-play event with around fifty competitors in the championship division and would have me playing six matches before making the finals. My first match was against a gentleman named Mitch Willow. Mitch lived on Long Island and had a 6 handicap. We were in the championship flight, so there were no handicaps, as everyone was equal, or so I thought. It turns out there were a few women in the tournament as well, and they had been given the advantage of playing the forward tees. I didn't mind this so much since my main purpose for being in this tournament was to see how my swing would hold up under the pressure of the golf course and in competition. I had spent the past few months in the comfort of the driving range. This tournament was the next step, just as a musician who spends his days practicing in solitude and then decides to play a recital in front of a crowd. I was there not only to compete but to showcase my art within the game of golf.

On the day of the match, I met Mitch at the clubhouse, and we made our introductions. He was a great guy, and we had some insightful conversations about golf. His game, however, was not anywhere near the level of mine. I won the match 8 and 7. I could tell Mitch was frustrated with how he played, so when I received a text from him the following week asking for a rematch, I was not surprised. I was surprised, though, when he challenged me to $5 a hole with no handicap strokes. I gladly accepted the challenge; if anything, this would be a fun round of golf with my new friend. I arrived at the golf course as both teacher and player. Mitch had already expressed an interest in my understanding and said he had a few questions and challenges for me. On the first hole, a short par-4, Mitch made a nice par, but it was of little consequence because I made a 6-foot putt for birdie. On the second hole, I made birdie again, as Mitch made par. I still had the feeling that Mitch thought he could compete with me, but that feeling would soon change. The third hole was a 165-yard par-3, which we both landed on in regulation. I two-putted and Mitch three-putted, which irritated him tremendously because he missed a small 3-footer.

On the way to the next tee, Mitch started asking some questions. He first asked me if there was anything at all I could give him to mechanically work on when he practiced. I told him that if I did that, he would no longer be working in a mental state of freedom, and all natural development would be lost. Embracing a free, clear mind—that should be the game plan, not learning mechanics. This seems to be very difficult for most people to grasp, but it is probably the most essential thing you can learn in this teaching. If a mechanical direction is given, then all creativity is lost and you become just a machine, performing the same action repeatedly.

"What I am trying to get you to understand, Mitch, is

that your brain is so intelligent, that if left alone to operate and learn independently, it will sort out all the issues that you now see affecting your swing. Most teachers want to study your swing and look for obvious correction—a bent left arm, alignment, sequence from the top of the swing, things of this nature. My issue with this type of teaching is this: How do you know that the 'correction' you are making is actually correct? And if you correct one thing, how does that correction affect the rest of the swing? The golf swing is not a machine as much as most teachers would have you believe. The golf swing is a living, human action, which means affecting one part of it will affect the whole structure, not just the part you seemingly fix."

I could see Mitch was wrestling with what I had just said. "Mitch, let's just keep playing and talk about this as we go along. I think the more we discuss what I am saying, the clearer the picture will become." On the next three holes, I went birdie, birdie, birdie, as I explained how we must have trust in the ability of the subconscious to figure out this game. I myself was only months into my own training but was already seeing huge changes in my swing and game. The seventh hole was a very long and challenging par-3, 222 yards from the back tees. I hit my 3 iron to six feet, while Mitch missed the green. Up to this point, I had been putting really well. As I approached the putt on No. 7, I felt as though I needed to make it because it was so close, and up to that point, most of the putts I made that day were all longer. As soon as I struck the putt, I could feel the conscious control take over, and I missed it. My frustration was obvious. I turned to Mitch and said, "I consciously caused that miss." He didn't understand what I was saying.

"You see, Mitch, the conscious mind has been conditioned over thousands of years. We have built our whole society on conscious control. We have been told to compete and to try and make things happen. Up until this point, I was not consciously trying. I was just allowing myself to express myself in whatever way my unconscious mind wanted. Standing over that putt, I was telling myself I needed to make that putt, therefore, putting undo pressure on myself." I explained to Mitch that true creativity and freedom could only come when an outcome of any kind was abandoned. One of my favorite quotes is: "Expectation is the mother of disappointment." Never was a statement more true. As we drove to the next hole, I knew I would not be looking for an outcome for the rest of the round. I would accept whatever the golf gods had in store for me. My experience had taught me that control was not the answer.

On the next hole, I had a similar length putt for birdie. I had no expectation of making it, and sure enough, in it went. I arrived at the ninth hole with a sense of confidence that I could trust this process even if I didn't totally understand it. My drive went left toward a big tree but landed safely underneath it. I had a shot left of around 150 yards. The ball was resting just under the branches of the tree, so a normal shot was not possible. I walked to the bag and pulled a 6 iron. My shot came out nice and low, then rose at the end, landing about fifteen feet from the hole. I approached the putt with the same awareness that I had all day. The putt lipped out, and I tapped in for a par. I finished the front side 6-under par, tying my all-time low for nine holes.

On holes ten and eleven, I had putts from just outside twenty feet for birdie, and after making both shots, I felt a sense of peace come over me. This was really turning into a hell of a round. I had never been this low before, but the pressure was not there as it usually was. I was too busy explaining to Mitch how this whole process worked. Over the next four holes, I only managed pars, missing two very short putts for birdies on two of them. It seemed that as I was playing, birdies were the norm and pars felt like bogeys.

I reached the sixteenth, which was a short but very tight

par-4. As I stood on the tee waiting for the group in front to clear the green, the group behind us pulled up. "We have a bet going that you are 7-under. Are we right?"

"Almost. I am 8 under right now," I said with a smile. Mitch kept shaking his head, saying how unreal it was what he was witnessing. This hole was only 292 yards but played downhill and was surrounded by out-of-bounds stakes, so if you're going to drive the green, you had better be accurate. A few weeks earlier with Preston, I drove the ball on the green and it ended up six inches away from a hole-in-one. So I knew I could hit the shot, but how would I perform now with everyone watching? I was not concerned with this. I really had no interest in shooting a number; I was more concerned with just making my swing. I stood over the ball in a state of utter clarity, and in a flash, the ball was gone, heading right at the flag. It took one bounce and stuck on the green, about 20 feet beyond the hole. All the players and onlookers stood in awe, congratulating me on the great shot. I missed the eagle putt but had a short tap-in for my ninth birdie of the day.

The seventeenth hole is a really great par-3, measuring 190 yards from the tips, but because of its severe uphill design, it played more like 210. I instantly grabbed a 4 iron and stood on the right side of the tee box. Now, this seemed a little strange to me, because the whole right side of the green is a death trap. If you land five feet right of the green, your ball will be O.B. But I trusted my instincts and my subconscious. Without a breath of fear, I said to myself, "OK, let's do this." I swung, and the ball took off with the most perfect little draw. Only minutes ago, the gentleman playing with us had said how he'd love to see a hole-in-one. As the ball was about halfway there, it looked as if he might get his wish. The ball landed just short of the pin and then disappeared. Being that we were below the green, we could not see the surface or the ball, so all we could do was wait until we reached the green. To me, it felt like one of the purest shots of the day, and I would not have been surprised if it went in. When we got to the green, there was the ball, about 13 feet past the hole on the low side. The pitch mark was about two feet short of the pin, right on line. That ball must have been so close to going in! Now it was time for me to make this putt. I walked into the putt, feeling as if the ball was already in. All I had to do was hit it. As the ball approached the hole, I started walking toward it, ready to pick the ball out of the bottom of the cup, but just then, it hit a spike mark, moved about a quarter-inch and did a full 360 around the cup! Everyone sighed, especially me. When I got to the cart to write the score, I started to circle the score to indicate a birdie, then I realized I had missed it. Wow, that was a great putt! As we pulled to eighteen, someone in the group said, "You do realize that if you eagle this final par-4, you'll shoot a 59." All day, for the most part, I hadn't really thought much about the score. I was more focused on showing Mitch how my new understanding operated and how he himself could improve his game by adopting this approach.

Now all I could think about was the 59. How many guys in the world get a chance to shoot a 59?! I went on to the eighteenth, a downhill 338-yard par-4 that I had reached in one a few weeks back. It would take a really amazing shot to reach the green, but I felt up to the task. The number "59" permeated my mind. Of course, I had to go for it. I might never get this chance again. My thoughts were almost obsessive at that point. I was going to will this shot whether my mind wanted it or not. During our match, Mitch had lost almost every hole to me and was now as focused as I was on this 59. He asked me if a driver was even necessary, being that I was hitting the ball so well today, and just over the back of the green was a whole bunch of shrubs and trouble. I told him that just last week, I hit a driver right on the center of the green from this same tee box, so this was the club to use. I struck the ball and off it went. The ball had a little pull to it but not that bad. Just

then, I remembered that on the left side of the green was the cart path. I couldn't see the ball land because the trees on the left blocked the view, but I had a feeling this might not turn out as I hoped. When I got down by the green, I thought I saw my ball in the left rough and immediately felt a sigh of relief. But that feeling soon faded as I approached the ball and realized it wasn't mine; it was a practice ball someone had left behind. I looked everywhere, but I knew what had happened: I had hit the cart path and the ball hopped over a small fence to the left of the green. I took a drop near the fence and was now lying two. I was not going to shoot my 59. My mind was out of it and clouded by disappointment. This didn't help when hitting the next chip shot. I duffed it maybe 10 feet and I was left lying three, still not on the green. I hit my next chip up close and that was it; the round was over. My final score was a 62, something to be proud of for sure, but I couldn't help shake the feeling that I gave away way too many shots on the final hole.

In the cart ride back to the clubhouse, I began telling Mitch that my only failure came on the last hole, in pursuit of that elusive 59. I allowed my desire for a result to determine my play off the tee. For nearly the entire round, I had not played for a score, but when immortality was in reach, I chose to sacrifice my freedom for the glory. Mitch thought I was being a bit dramatic and hard on myself, but to me, this was a very serious moment. I did not trust that my freedom and creativity would give me all I needed to finish the round, and, therefore, I experienced firsthand what my desire for an outcome could do. I left the course humbled that day, humbled by the fact that my true potential was cut short by one hole. But I also left content, knowing I was becoming a true master of not only my game but myself.

As we got back to the clubhouse I went to tell Jeff, the clubhouse manager, that I shot a 62. He asked for the scorecard, saying this might be a new course record! I had never even considered going for the course record when I began playing that day. This was to be purely a day of discovery and freedom. And there I was at the end of the day, quite possibly holding the course record! Jeff said he thought the record was a 63, but he needed to check to make sure. He would get back to me by the end of the week.

Mitch ponied up the $60 he lost and said he was more than happy to pay me after I shot that good of a round. He also said it was a real joy to watch, for which I thanked him. I told him that if he needed more convincing that my teaching worked, I would be happy to play him anytime. We both laughed and said our goodbyes. That was my lowest round ever, but in the end, it was never officially acknowledged. The following week, I called the pro shop to ask Jeff if I now held the course record. He went on to explain that the course record was indeed 63, as he thought, but my round didn't qualify, because on the eighteenth hole, I didn't go back to the tee and re-hit. Didn't qualify?! What a letdown. The fence behind the green is O.B., but I took a drop and played it like a lateral hazard. That mistake cost me, but then again, I wasn't there to shoot a number. I was there to paint a beautiful picture, and during that round, I truly painted a masterpiece.

CHAPTER 28

Freedom is not worth having if it does not include the freedom to make mistakes
– Mahatma Gandhi

NEWS OF MY 62 SPREAD like wildfire among all the competitors still left in the club championship. I had become a marked man and was now the odds-on favorite to win the championship. I had never been in this position before. I had always been a solid player but never drew much attention to myself. I was only a little over four months into my training when I shot the 62. As you can imagine, my nerves started to act up waiting for my next match to begin. I was no longer under the radar; I was Mr. 62 DQ (disqualified).

My next opponent was a woman named Katy. She had beaten a friend of mine, Teddy, in the first round of the tournament, which we unmercifully teased him about. He got beat by a girl! "Guys, I was spraying the ball that day and she was puring it right down the middle every time. Not to mention she was playing from the women's tees," Teddy said, trying to defend his manhood. We didn't care; we still let him have it.

The day of the match came, and I arrived at the first tee a little apprehensive about playing the woman who had beaten

Teddy. He had shot 68 the week before so my thinking was that Katy must be reasonably good to have beaten him. I introduced myself at the first tee and shook Katy's hand. Her response was cold; she would not even look me in the eye. I found this odd to say the least. What I had not realized, because I had never been in that position before, was that Katy was putting her game face on because I was the guy who shot 62 and I was most likely the best player remaining in the field. This meant if she could beat me, she would have a real chance of advancing to the finals. I found Katy's stoic demeanor ironic, as this was the same attitude I presented when playing against noteworthy golfers.

I teed off on No. 1 and, as usual, hit the ball right up next to the green with my driver. Katy went up to the women's tees, which I had never paid much attention to until that day. She was teeing off about 70 yards in front of me. Instantly, my brain looked at the scorecard. Was she going to be getting a 70-yard advantage all day? Yup, she sure was. In fact, she would be getting a 1,300-yard advantage. From the tips, this course was only 6,100 yards, so to spot someone that much yardage was, in my opinion, just plain crazy. Katy proceeded to hit her tee shot, which flew dead straight about 250 yards, right next to my ball. I immediately felt a bit of fear creep in. Katy might just beat me! She had some game, and I was not prepared for that.

Instead of focusing on playing my game and just enjoying the day, I was edgy and complaining to myself about Katy getting this huge distance advantage. Since I had begun my training, I had never played with anyone who could hit the ball as far as I could. All of my length advantage was gone, and it was now evident that I had a real match on my hands. I had made a truly fatal flaw; I had underestimated my opponent. Now I was seeing firsthand why Teddy had lost, and I was a bit nervous. By the eighth hole, I was down one and really upset. I had just missed a four-foot putt for birdie on eight to tie the match. I had real concern coming into nine, down by one. The ninth was one of those holes where I just never hit good shots on. I

ended up snuggling a forty-foot putt to about one foot, which tied the hole with Katy. I was one down heading into the back nine.

It was at that moment, on the drive from the ninth to the tenth hole, that I asked myself a very simple question: Why was I nervous? The simple answer was: Because I didn't want to lose to a girl! I picked on Teddy for losing to her and told all my friends not to worry, this one was in the bag. Now the fact that I was down one with only nine holes to play made me worried. I was aware that being beaten by a woman was nothing to be ashamed of. In fact, I was pretty sure a whole slew of women could beat me on any given day. I had more ups and downs than a Ferris wheel in my game.

I had to remind myself that I wasn't there to solely win a golf tournament; I was there to bring a new understanding to golf and see if it would work. This whole round, I was doing just the opposite: I was stressing, not accepting, the outcome. If the outcome was a loss, then so be it. It was then, after this realization, that my disposition changed and so did my game. I looked at Katy and smiled, told her she did a nice job on that side and it was well played. She was silent and in total focus. I became free and no longer felt any fear. I hit my tee shot and instantly knew Katy's chances of beating me were over. I was back to creating from a space of awareness and freedom. Katy, on the other hand, was solely focused on winning. The problem with that type of focus is this: When you set a goal of winning and focus only on that, you shut yourself off from being in your most creative state. The mind isn't fluid or open to new ideas or possibilities. You steer away from anything that risks failure; therefore, you are not in a state of freedom. It's necessary to embrace the possibility of failure, because it allows you to grow and learn and, most importantly, gives you a certain clarity that only a free mind can see.

I let go of my results-driven mentality and just allowed myself to have fun and be creatively expressive. As soon as that change in attitude and mindset occurred, I began hitting superior shots that Katy could no longer compete with. She was consciously guiding her shots toward an expectation, limiting her mindset; whereas, I released that pressure from myself and trusted my ability and my subconscious to guide me. One way is freedom, the other is not.

The match ended on the fifteenth hole. Katy shook my hand, and I could literally feel her disappointment. I told her I was very impressed with her playing and that I was not prepared for such a great test. She said she didn't take advantage when she had the chance in the beginning. I agreed that I was very vulnerable for the first nine holes and felt lucky to only be one down heading into the back nine.

Once our match was over, Katy's whole demeanor changed; she became very friendly and chatty, and I could see all the pressure that she had been carrying the entire round just wash away. I honestly had compassion for her, and it made me question the very nature of competition. I had always harnessed a great disdain for the tension and anxiety that competition evoked. This was something I struggled with from an early age. My father, during all of his years caddying for me, would often say, "Why are you playing so bad? This is no different than just playing with me on the weekend." But to me it was different; I was playing against pros and for my honor. I was always trying to prove myself in competition, and by doing so, my mind and attitude became less fluid. This mentality was the very reason I had never excelled to my full potential … until now. I was beginning to realize that competition was not the problem; the problem was my approach to competition. And my new understanding and teaching were helping me grasp this. I wanted to bring a different approach to competition in golf—one that allowed both the mind and body to be in sync with each other and excel in a state of clarity and creativity.

CHAPTER 29

The ability to observe without evaluating is the highest form of intelligence
– Jiddu Krishnamurti

My next opponent in the club championship was a Latin gentleman named Gil. He stood about 6-feet-2, was around 50 years old, and had a short game like no one I had ever seen. I wasn't about to make the same mistake I had with Katy and underestimate my opponent. On the first hole, Gil hit the ball right behind a tree, while I was a wedge away from the pin. I took the first and second holes to gain a quick lead. I would soon witness why he was a better player than his start indicated. Sure enough, once his nerves relaxed and he started finding the fairway, Gil was nearly unstoppable. I would be 30 yards ahead of him, but he almost never missed getting up and down, even chipping in a few times. By the time we reached the ninth hole, the match was all square. This was a very important match, as the winner would be in the finals the following week. But I never let that thought enter my mind. I was focused on keeping my mind quiet and simply allowing the subconscious to guide me. There was no pressure, but I could see just by the shots Gil was hitting that my short game needed work. He had such creativity around the green, and being that I was not overthinking or analyzing things, but instead just observing, I was able to learn from Gil and discover shots that I never knew existed.

Observation is a vital part of the learning process. As children, we learn to walk, ride a bike, throw a ball, or perform any other motor skill by observing how others do it. We initiate the learning process by mimicking what we see. If our parents have good posture and are athletes, we are more prone to those good habits and becoming athletes ourselves. Of course, the necessary practice and due diligence must also be performed if we are to excel. All of this leads to the flowering of the unknown.

This, of course, was all very speculative and could be coincidence, but the more I looked around, the more I saw it to be true. If you want to excel, you need to have people around who are at the top of their game and with whom to study. I realized that Gil had new movements to show my brain, and if I was alert and attentive, it would pick up all these great short-game shots. I watched him as closely as I could, never analyzing his swing with thought but, instead, just giving him my full, silent attention. I was able to defeat Gil on the seventeenth hole after he made his only poor chip of the day and I made a short putt. We shook hands, and I thanked him for a great round and for showing me shots I had not yet known. He told me that I deserved the championship match and that I had all the shots required to be a champion.

CHAPTER 30

To be yourself in a world that is constantly trying to make you something else is the greatest accomplishment
– Ralph Waldo Emerson

I HAD MADE IT to the finals. I felt that I was at my peak in both mental and physical training. All of the previous matches leading up to this pivotal moment had a significant impact on me. Never underestimate my opponent; adopt a fluid mentality; simply observe without judgment—all of these lessons had strengthened me as a player both in mind and body. Golf is more of a mental game than most sports. If your mind is not in a state of freedom, your game will reflect that imbalance, and it will suffer. My game was in top form, and my mind had reached its ultimate clarity. I was ready for this.

I went the very next day to the range to practice my short game, as that's what needed the most attention. The championship match was less than a week away. As I was practicing, I got a phone call from Michael Forest, my opponent for the final match. Due to a family emergency, he needed to fly to Buffalo, New York, on Wednesday and would not be back in time for the match the following Monday. He asked if we could play tomorrow. Otherwise, he would be forced to forfeit the match. This was extremely short notice, and I had mentally prepared myself to play in a week's time, not the very next day! I had hoped to practice all week and play the following Monday, when players and spectators would be there to watch us. This, instead, would be just the two of us playing first thing in the morning.

True, it was not as I had planned or expected. But this was the perfect moment to put my fluid mentality to practice. I needed to look at the situation as it was and make it work for me. Besides, I didn't want to win this trophy by default. I was a gentleman and an honorable player. I would win this championship because I was the best golfer. I told Michael I would see him first thing in the morning.

I awoke the next day feeling incredibly nervous. This was the farthest I had ever gotten in any golf tournament, and the reality of it all was starting to sink in. When I signed up for this event, I had no real expectation of winning. But here I was, playing for the Van Cortlandt club championship. I left my apartment early in the morning and hopped on the subway. I had about a 40-minute commute to the course, which gave me plenty of time to think. That was the worst thing in the world for me. I started feeling sick and thinking about how it would look if I lost. My mind was racing with "what-if" thoughts, and I was really psyching myself out. I decided that maybe if I started writing about what I was feeling, I could find something that would help calm me down. The following is what I wrote in that moment:

So here I am in the finals at the club championship at Van Cortlandt. My brain is racing, looking for a way or a method to approach this round. The mind is scared, scared that it won't perform—that the pressure will be too great. The mind is a bundle of incomplete memories drawing from the past in order to deal with the present moment. The mind must be still in order to function at its highest possible level. I cannot force the mind into stillness, for then I will be in conflict, and conflict indicates confusion. A mind that sees its own confusion is no longer confused.

That is the only requirement: to see your mind's movements and see that its confusion is caused by using thought. Once the mind sees this, it no longer pursues thought. When the mind truly sees this, quietness comes into being without any effort. The fact is, I have trained very hard for this day. All the skills required to play well are there. Nothing more than that fact is required. The outcome is what it is. How we arrive at that outcome has yet to be determined. If my full awareness is given to the task at hand, then all my faculties are available. If my mind starts imagining or analyzing the situation, then my approach will be limited and failure will most certainly be a possibility. My mind is so clear at this moment; it feels as if the words are writing themselves much in the way I feel when golf is played at the highest level. There is no method that will give freedom, because a method implies control and control is never freedom. It is only in freedom that one can express their full potential. Today I will play in freedom.

As soon as I finished writing this passage, I was in a state of true effortlessness and love. It wasn't elicited or forced, as it had seemed all those years ago when I was so inclined to be in an effortless state. This time was different. This was natural, not forced. If something is forced, it is in a state of imbalance. This required no force at all. I walked off the train in a state of true emotional bliss. As I strolled through the park to the course, I started to tear up. I'm not sure why I was moved to tears, but I do know it wasn't out of pain but, instead, was a joyous feeling. I felt the greatest sense of love I had ever experienced and knew that life was about to show me something special if I would just let it.

Michael was already at the clubhouse when I arrived, and we made our introductions. We reached the first tee just as the sun was cresting the trees. It was the most beautiful sunrise I had ever seen. Michael went first and striped a driver right down the middle, about forty yards from the green. I heard that he was a long hitter, and being that he was probably only 26 years old, he had plenty of flexibility on this chilly September morning. As I walked toward my bag, I was in a clear state of awareness and love; my eyes immediately locked on my 5 iron. The irony was that I had played this course maybe thirty times, and each of those times, I grabbed the driver, never the 5 iron. I had never knocked it on the green from here, but I had been on the fringe a few times. Now my brain, in a state of ultimate clarity, wanted a 5 iron. I didn't hesitate; I took the 5 and hit it dead center to the 150-yard marker. In the fairway, I took a 9 iron, which was also an unconventional selection, as it was cold and the pin was all the way back, leaving me with about a 165-yard shot. I took my swing with confidence, watching the ball sail and land 10 feet short of the green. I was not fazed one bit.

Michael hit his shot to eight feet, for a seemingly easy birdie. I approached my chip and without a breath of hesitation, struck a low spinning wedge. The ball landed, took two hops, and dropped straight in the hole. I didn't even react; I just walked up, took my ball out of the hole, and pulled the pin. Michael missed his putt, and I knew right then the match was over. He thought he was going to have a one-hole lead after No. 1, only to watch me steal it right from under his nose. His confidence was broken, and he never recovered. I won the match 4 and 5. We both shook hands and he congratulated me on the win. I had just won the Van Cortlandt club championship.

When we returned to the clubhouse, Jeff, the pro shop manager, anxiously asked how the match went. Michael smiled a bit and said, "It was fun, but I'm not in the same league as this gentleman. He is a true champion." I was humbled. Love and freedom, coupled with years of physical preparation, had taken me from being the last-place player on my high school golf team to the club champion at the oldest, most historic public course in America. No tournament would ever mean more to me than this one. I could not wait to share the good news with everyone and express what freedom had done

for me. I called my girlfriend, Jennifer, but before I even said a word, she told me she knew I had won; she had felt it all morning. It was clear to everyone who knew me that I was making huge steps in my game. Now I had all the proof I needed for myself. Here I was, only six months into this year of training, and I was seeing things happen in my game I never could have imagined. I had nearly advanced through local qualifying in the U.S. Open, placed fourteenth in the Maine Open, nearly shot a 59, and just won the Van Cortlandt club championship. I had truly discovered a new way to play golf and for the first time in my life, I felt at peace with the game.

The following week, I received my trophy at the club championship dinner and benefit. The whole staff and all of the players congratulated me. It was an amazing feeling to see all my hard work validated. At the conclusion of the night, a raffle was held for a tall locker in the clubhouse. I had hoped that by winning the club championship, I would automatically be awarded the locker, but that wasn't the case. I was left to hope that my number would be called just like everyone else. The reason I was so eager to get this locker was because the Van Cortlandt locker room, just like the course, had a lot of history. It had been used by greats such as Babe Ruth, the Three Stooges and countless other celebrities throughout its history. It was even used as the locker room in the movie "Wall Street." The waiting list to get a locker was as long as a par-5, because everyone wanted to leave their clubs at the course. The number 00186 was called, and before I even got my hand in my pocket to check my number, a gentleman yelled out, "That's ME!" They checked his ticket and told him that he had 01866, not the right ticket. They announced the ticket again, and another gentlemen said he was the winner. He, too, was mistaken. This was getting a bit ridiculous, if not amusing. I looked at Preston and told him that I still hadn't bothered to look at my ticket. As I reached in my pocket and looked at the number, I could not believe what I was seeing. I had the winning ticket! The whole place went nuts! Not only had I won the Van Cortlandt club champion trophy, I now also had a locker to hold it in! I was truly a blessed man, and freedom was now the focal point in my life and game.

I had just finished six months of playing in absolute freedom; not effortless freedom or any other form of control. Freedom was the only way I would ever play again and now I felt I could share my discoveries with others. I was finally ready to embrace being the teacher I had always been but was too afraid to accept. I decided after this whole experience to begin writing this book, so I could leave a record of what had happened. It would be a way for me to help others question the very meaning of the word "freedom" and, hopefully, challenge people to look inside themselves and discover their full potential. I hope this offering makes you ask that same question I asked myself all those years ago: What would happen if you had no ideas or beliefs about how to swing a golf club?

If you do, maybe you will find the same peace I found with golf.

EPILOGUE

I HOPE THAT by reading this book, you can see what is involved in learning to become a golfer in freedom. My goal was to show golfers what could be done if the game, and life, were looked at from a different perspective. I wanted to show how traditional teaching is a long, drawn-out process and how freedom and creativity are an exploration into the unknown, always alive and full of hidden treasures. This book is to help golfers of all ages and abilities reach their full potential and challenge their current beliefs and ideas. It has all the information needed for someone of any level to open the door of creativity and see behind that door into the unknown realm of freedom. I wish all readers good fortune on the links and in life. With all my love to everyone in the world—keep your drives long and straight, and your mind clear with the freshness of a child. Good luck to all and feel free to reach out any time to challenge my understanding. For without your own inquiries, we all become followers, and followers never discover the truth for themselves.

ACKNOWLEDGMENTS

This book was made after many years of hard work in the game of golf. I certainly put in the physical labor of training myself but without the help of a few key people this book may have never seen the light of day:

My parents, who gave me their unconditional love and support toward my golf career. At every point in my life you have both been there for me. Thank you for always allowing me to be myself.

Jennifer, my loving girlfriend and best friend. I could have never done it without you. Seriously, never.

Mr. David Lee, my first real golf coach, and his family. Without their support and love I certainly would have never turned out to be the golfer I am today. David- your willingness to challenge the status quo and develop your own style was the impetus for me to find my own way and write this book.

Uncle Mark- you were right- the real work begins after you write the book!

My Broadway friends and colleagues – you know who you are - your patience, advice, and support were instrumental on this journey.

Special thanks to all the golfers who have helped me learn about the game and myself. With love and peace, I say once again...thank you to all who helped me arrive at this point.

ABOUT THE AUTHOR

Noah Pilipski is the founder of Peaceful-Golf. He has been teaching golf since 1999 and has won numerous awards for his teaching. Noah has been featured in both Golf Magazine and Golf Digest, along with other noteworthy publications. He has been seen on television around the world and continues to share his message of peace and freedom everywhere he goes. He currently lives in New York City.